On This Journey

Prayer Journal for Young People

On This Journey

On This Journey

Prayer Journal for Young People

By

Rev. Onedia N. Gage

Books by

Onedia N. Gage

Are You Ready for 9th Grade . . . Again? A Family's Guide to Success
As We Grow Together Daily Devotional for Expectant Couples
As We Grow Together Prayer Journal for Expectant Couples
The Best 40 Days of Your Life: A Journey of Spiritual Renewal
The Blue Print: Poetry for the Soul
From Two to One: The Notebook for the Christian Couple
Her Story: Bible Study
Her Story: Daily Devotional
Her Story: The Legacy of Her Fight
Her Story: The Legacy Journal
Her Story: Prayers and Journal
ILY! A Mother Daughter Success Kit
In Her Own Words: Notebook for the Christian Woman
In Purple Ink: Poetry for the Spirit
The Intensive Retreat for Couples for Her
The Intensive Retreat for Couples for Him
Living a Whole Life: Sermons which Promote, Prompt and Provoke Life
Love Letters to God from a Teenage Girl
The Measure of a Woman: The Details of Her Soul
The Notebook: For Me, About Me, By Me
The Notebook for the Christian Teen
On This Journey Daily Devotional for Young People
On This Journey Prayer Journal for Young People
One Day More Than We Deserve Daily Devotional for the Growing Christian
One Day More Than We Deserve Prayer Journal for the Growing Christian
Promises, Promises: A Christian Novel
Queen in the Making: Girls Rites of Passage
Tools for These Times: Timely Sermons for Uncertain Times
With An Anointed Voice: The Power of Prayer
Yielded and Submitted: A Woman's Journey for a Life Dedicated to God
Yielded and Submitted: A Woman's Journey for a Life Dedicated to God Intimate Study
Yielded and Submitted: A Woman's Journey for a Life Dedicated to God Prayers and Journal

Library of Congress

On This Journey
Prayer Journal for Young People

All Rights Reserved © 2004. 2015
by Onedia N. Gage

No part of this book may be reproduced or transmitted in any part of form or by any means, graphic, electronic or mechanical, including photocopying, recording, taping, or by any information storage of retrieval system, without the permission in writing from the publisher.

For information, please contact:
Purple Ink, Inc.
P O Box 41232
Houston, TX 77241
www.purpleink.net
onediagage@purpleink.net

Onedia Gage Ministries
www.onediagage.com
onediagage@onediagage.com

ISBN 978-09801002-1-1

Printed in the United States

What God Said

Be anxious for nothing, but in everything by prayer and supplication with thanksgiving let your requests be made to God.
                        Philippians 4:6 NAS

In the same way, the Spirit helps us in our weakness. We do not know what we ought to pray for, but the Spirit himself intercedes for us with groans that words cannot express.
                        Romans 8:26 NIV

Until now you have not asked for anything in my name. Ask and you will receive, and your joy will be complete.
                        John 16:24 NIV

Dedication

Hillary Nicole, may these words guide and motivate you to be faithful to God and the path He has planned for you. Lean on Him and depend on Him for all of your needs. When I started this project, I didn't know you would be born before I was finished. I love you and will always be here for you.

Nehemiah Christian, may these words inspire you to honor God through who you are. God has great plans for you. I look forward to the great works He has planned for you and through you. You were born before we printed this, so I am excited to have you here. I love you and will always be here for you.

To our children—our gifts from God—If I pray for you, then you will remain strong.

To my prayer warriors, may all of our prayers be answered.

To the youth whose lives this will touch: may these words inspire you to respond to God's calling. Keep your relationship with God healthy. May these words inspire you to desire to achieve the level God has planned for you. My prayers are for you daily.

Dear Hillary Nicole:

When I started writing this devotional in 1999, I had only dreamed of you—my little girl. I wrote this for you and now that you are here, I am so excited. I read and talk to you about God all the time. I pray over you everyday. I love you and your healthy spiritual wellness is extremely important to me.

When you are old enough to read this, I urge you to ask as many questions as you need. I am right here for you as your example of Christianity and your biggest supporter.

You will encounter things—all of which I may not mention specifically—for which I have prepared you. At that time, it may not seem as if I have but you are prepared and most importantly you are covered with my prayers and God's protection.

May the Lord bless you and keep you. May the light of His countenance shine on you and give you His peace. May He bless you as you go out and come in; rise early and settle late; in your labor and your leisure; in your laughter and in your tears.

I love you always!

Love,

Mommy
Onedia N. Gage

On This Journey

Dear Nehemiah Christian:

When I finished this project and was ready to print, you were due. I was excited for you to finally be here. I read and talk to you about God all the time. I pray over you everyday. I love you and your healthy spiritual wellness is extremely important to me.

When you are old enough to read this, I urge you to ask as many questions as you need. I am right here for you as your example of Christianity and your biggest supporter.

You will encounter things –all of which I may not mention specifically—for which I have prepared you. At that time, it may not seem as if I have but you are prepared and most importantly you are covered with my prayers and God's protection.

May the Lord bless you and keep you. May the light of His countenance shine on you and give you His peace. May He bless you as you go out and come in; rise early and settle late; in your labor and your leisure; in your laughter and in your tears.

I love you always!

Love,

Mommy
Onedia N. Gage

Dear Teen Christian:

It is awesome you've selected *On This Journey Prayer Journal for Young People* for use as your personal journal. Your study of God's word is extremely important. Your intimate time with God is equally as important. *OTJ* will help you remain consistent with your time dedicated to God. I started on a journey with Christ at a very early age. I accepted Jesus as my Lord and Savior at age 8. Our journey has been one full of excitement and discovery. I have excited and disappointed God in my life. I have learned a lot, too.

Each day is dated such that you may start as soon as you receive your journal. Each day starts with a scripture and ends with a prayer. The space is for your expressions to God and what God is telling you. This is your time with God. Your intimacy level is affected by the quality time spent. This is not a diary but a prayer journal for the prayers you have, inclusive of your desires, petitions, pleas, and thanksgiving.

I wrote *OTJ* because biblical resources for youth are limited and young people need resources to succeed. As a young person, I struggled to find resources to help me with my walk with God. I didn't want my child or others to have the same trouble. *OTJ* allows you the freedom to express yourself to God and not limit yourself to answering questions. This journal is the personal documentation and will not resemble another's. Feel free to express yourself in anyway the Lord leads you. Keep a list of your prayers to God so that when He answers you will know He has answered you. Often, Christians assume that God has ignored us, but He has not forgotten our plea, nor our desires, not even our needs. We were the ones who forgot. God doesn't forget our prayers—not even the little ones.

You should expect to spend 30 minutes daily: 10 minutes to read and 20 minutes writing in your journal. You also need to make time to pray, which may last two minutes or ten minutes. You and God will determine that time. You also should expect to address your issues in a new and honest way. For example, you may not have known how to talk to God before but now you'll know better about your conversations with God. Your growth and maturity will demand a new attitude about God, His word, your commitment, inclusive of your study time, prayer life and lifestyle.

My prayer for you daily is that God blesses you beyond measure, cover you in His love and give you the desires of your heart. I also ask for your increased growth, maturity, knowledge and enlightenment through your increased study and commune with God. May you follow the direction and guidance of the Holy Spirit. I pray that God forgives you according to His word rather than what we deserve.

I pray that you are patient when God doesn't answer you when you want Him to. I pray He grant you favor when you encounter storms and uncertain times. I pray for grace for you when you don't understand God's work, will and plan. I pray for mercy for you when you question God and when we deserve worse than what He does. Overall, I pray God's continued anointing of you and your ventures. I pray that God's love continue to embrace you and motivate you to achieve your dreams. In your youthfulness and folly, I pray God forgive you for any youthful indiscretions. I also pray He show you how to forgive yourself for any mistakes you make.

Just a last note, 1 Thessalonians 5:17, Matthew 5:44 and Luke 6:28 are all scriptures which address prayer, its importance, and His expectations of prayer. When in doubt, seek His face. He will reveal Himself and answers you will never anticipate.

If you should need to reach me for questions, prayer or additional resources, please email me at onediagage@purpleink.net or onediagage@onediagage.com.

In Christ,

Onedia Gage

Onedia N. Gage

Dear Parent:

A letter from my mother follows. I just implore you as a parent to be attentive to your child, especially when they are highly inquisitive and precocious. Embrace their ideas and listen to them, even when you don't want to. They need your validation of who they are and whose they are. This validation stretches you in ways you may be unprepared to explore but without fear, I encourage your obedience as you approach the challenges your child presents. Your validity of them changes their life and strongly impacts their choices, leading them to what's right and away from what's wrong.

Life outside the parental box is far from easy. My short parenting journey thus far has proved interesting but doesn't make me and expert. Not even close. However, it does allow me to reflect on the type of child I was. Further, my childhood forces me to pray and ask my mother for forgiveness. Getting out of the box is required. First, abandoning the box means you are free to parent according to God's words. This means parenting with discipline and love and prayer, among other Christ-centered qualities and behaviors.

Secondly, the box is not good for neither parent nor child. Consider parenting to please the society and your child rather than using God's word as your source for instruction. The Bible clearly defines the parental role. So is the child's. So the child cannot be in their role if you are not properly functioning within yours. Without the correct roles, friction, disobedience and discords results.

Lastly, the box presents a false sense of security and self-esteem. It also gives the illusion you have done the right thing. We compare our parenting to other parents rather than the Bible. This comparison gives a skewed snapshot of someone else's parental report card, if you will. The problem is that the next parents are presented with similar challenges as we ask them how they handled it then we decide what to do. This approach is disorderly. We are to ask God, refer to His Instructions and wait on His answer.

By the way, just because we made a better decision than another parent is not grounds for celebration. We need to pray for each other that we are able to present to strong, united, Christ-centered front. It is safe to discard the "box." God does not operate in that box. He does not want us in the box but will allow us in our time to discard the "box." Just a tip I learned from the wise woman who mothered me: 'so if she jumps off the bridge, are you going to jump, too?' I stopped using others to persuade my mother for things I wanted. Stop listening to what others do.

If you have any questions, are in need of prayer, or need more resources, please email me at onediagage@onediagage.com.

In Christ,

Onedia N. Gage

Dear Parents:

When my youngest daughter asked me to write a letter about parenting, I truly laughed. Then she said she was serious. My question was 'and who am I to discuss parenting,' but she persisted. So here goes.

The two most important jobs we do in this life do not require training or classes. Parenting is the second, with the first one being choosing a mate. I felt that I always struggled with my girls. I loved them but never did the hugging and such. I let my outside relationships, job, financial concerns, etc., interfere with my relationship, reactions and responses to them. Looking back, I thank God daily that they are as well as they are.

Now I know that I would do some things differently. Let children know you love them. They do not have to be perfect to be loved nor do you for them to love you. They do not know how the perfect parent looks, so go for it. Just be honest with yourself and with them too.

Just enjoy your children and time together. Cherish the silly fun things and learn to laugh. Life is too hard to be so serious. Make memories every time you get the chance and relive them often for the growth of everybody. We forget if we do not rehearse often.

Then pray. The Word will give you the direction and strength you need to meet the situations you face with children. Then when they ask why and howcome, you can have a strong comeback, with Biblical principles. This is needed especially for dealing with the strong-willed child. This will give you confidence and courage; so do not resign no matter what. When your child at age two decides not to sing the correct words to the song as you tell them to her then, you know you need lots of support and direction.

And now that both of the girls have children, I just laugh at everything the grandchildren do, and tell the parents, "the apple does not fall far from the tree."

Sincerely,

Onedia W. Carroll
"The Mommy"

TABLE OF CONTENTS

Dedication	11
Letters	13
Why Prayer is Important	22
January	23
February	54
March	83
Developing Your Prayer Life—Part One	114
April	115
May	147
June	178
Developing Your Prayer Life—Part Two	209
July	210
August	241
September	272
Reading God's Word	302
October	303
November	334
December	364
God's Answers to Your Prayers	396
Resources for the Journey	397

WHY PRAYER IS IMPORTANT

Prayer is communication to God. Prayer is how we confess our sins and express our adoration, our fears, our desires, our needs, our everything to God. Prayer is one way God communicates with you, too. Prayer brings you to closer to God.

I Thessalonians 5:17 reads "pray continually." All the time. At every occasion. Prayer at meals is important, too as Jesus set forth that as important and led by example (John 6:11).

The following scriptures are about prayer: Matthew 5:44; 6:5-15; 26:36, 39-42; Luke 6:28; 18:1; 22:40; Romans 8:26; Mark 11:22-26; James 5:13-16; Philippians 4:6; and Ephesians 6:18-20.

These scriptures give instruction, encouragement and advice about prayer. Jesus is the leader of the movement and its importance. Jesus prayed to His Father for all occasions and is honest in His requests. God is true to His word and will hear and answer you.

Prayer can also be a period of praise and worship. Prayer is an integral instrument of your spiritual growth and maturity.

Prayer is critically important for your spiritual survival. Prayer feeds your spirit and fuels your soul.

… Prayre Jornnal for Young People

JANUARY 1

³And God said, "Let there be light," and there was light.

Git... *Genesis 1:3*

___

Thank You, God for Your creation.

JANUARY 2

[4]You shall not make for yourself an idol in the form of anything in heaven above or the earth beneath or in the waters below.

Exodus 20:4 - 6

_____
_____
_____
_____
_____
_____
_____
_____
_____
_____
_____
_____
_____
_____
_____
_____
_____
_____
_____
_____
_____
_____
_____
_____
_____
_____
_____
_____
_____
_____

Lord, I only want to worship You.

JANUARY 3

[7] You shall not misuse the name of the Lord your God, for the Lord will not hold anyone guiltless who misuses His name.

Exodus 20:7

Lord, thank You for the privilege to call Your name.

JANUARY 4

[8]Remember the Sabbath day by keeping it holy.

Exodus 20:8-11

God, keep me Holy whether the Sabbath or not.

JANUARY 5

[12] Honor your father and your mother, so that you may live long in the land the Lord your God is giving you.

Exodus 20:12

Thank You Lord, for my parents, biological and spiritual.

JANUARY 6

¹³You shall not murder.

Exodus 20:13

Lord, help me forgive those who've murdered. Lord, forgive those who've committed suicide.

JANUARY 7

[14]You shall not commit adultery.

Exodus 20:14

Lord, help me honor my commitment.

JANUARY 8

[15]You shall not steal.

Exodus 20:15

Father, forgive those who have stolen.

Prayre Jornnal for Young People

JANUARY 9

[16]You shall not give false testimony against your neighbor.

Exodus 20:16

Lord, guide my tongue such that I don't falsely accuse my neighbor.

JANUARY 10

[17]You shall not covet your neighbor's house. You shall not covet your neighbor's wife, or his manservant or maidservant, his ox or donkey, or anything that belongs to your neighbor.

Exodus 20:17

Remember, "What God has for me is for me."

JANUARY 11

[24]The Lord bless you and keep you. [25]The Lord make His face shine upon you and be gracious to you. [26]The Lord turn His face toward you and give you peace.

Numbers 6:24-26

_____

Lord, thank You for Your blessings.

JANUARY 12

[16]When all our enemies heard about this, all the surrounding nations were afraid and lost their self-confidence, because they realized that this work had been done with the help of our God.

Nehemiah 6:16

___

Lord, they may not have accepted You personally, but they respect Your power even from afar.

JANUARY 13

⁶You alone are the Lord. You made the heavens; even the highest heavens, and all their starry hosts. The earth and all that is on it. The seas and all that is in them. You give life to everything, and the multitudes of heaven worship you.

Nehemiah 9:6

Thank You, Father God for presence and authority over this world. Thank You for my life.

JANUARY 14

[13]You came down on Mount Sinai; you spoke to them from heaven. You gave them regulations and laws that are just and right, and decrees and commands that are good.

Nehemiah 9:13

_____
_____
_____
_____
_____
_____
_____
_____
_____
_____
_____
_____
_____
_____
_____
_____
_____
_____
_____
_____
_____
_____
_____
_____
_____
_____
_____
_____
_____

Lord, help me follow Your laws and decrees. I will obey because of my respect and love for You.

JANUARY 15

[4]To the Lord I cry aloud, and he answers me from his holy hill.

Psalm 3:4

Lord, thank You for answering my plea.

JANUARY 16

[1]O Lord, our Lord, how majestic is your name in all the earth! You have set your glory above the heavens.

Psalm 8:1

Lord, thank You for Your overwhelming presence.

JANUARY 17

[1]God is our refuge and our strength, an ever present help in trouble.

Psalm 46:1

Lord, thank You for Your strength and Your refuge.

JANUARY 18

[10]Be still and know that I am God; I will be exalted among the nations, I will be exalted in the earth.

Psalm 46:10

Lord, help me be still and to seek Your face.

JANUARY 19

[2]Hear my prayer, O God: listen to the words of my mouth.

Psalm 54:2

Lord, listening to the words that come out of my mouth is a powerful demonstration of Your love for me. Thank You.

JANUARY 20

Fear and trembling have beset me; honor has overwhelmed me.

Psalm 55:5

Lord, I fear that I will disobey and sin beyond Your ability to forgive me. Lord, calm my fears, I pray.

JANUARY 21

[16]But I call to God, and the Lord saves me.

Psalm 55:16

Lord, thank You for saving me when I call, especially from myself.

JANUARY 22

[3] When I am afraid, I will trust in you.

Psalm 56:3

Lord, I will seek You when I can't see.

JANUARY 23

[1]My soul finds rest in God alone; my salvation comes from Him.

Psalm 62:1

Father, thank You for rest.

JANUARY 24

[2]He alone is my rock and my salvation; he's my fortress, I will never be shaken,

Psalm 62:2

God, thank You for salvation and stability.

JANUARY 25

[1]O God, you are my God, earnestly I seek you; my soul thirsts for you, my body longs for you, in a dry and weary land where there is no water.

Psalm 63:1

Master, I come humbly seeking You for rest of my soul, peace in my thoughts, and rest for my body.

JANUARY 26

[8] My soul clings to you; your right hand upholds me.

Psalm 63:8

Father, my soul clings to You because it is of You and is not subject to flesh.

JANUARY 27

[7]In your distress you called and I rescued you, I answered you out of a thunder cloud; I tested you at the waters at Meribah.

Psalm 81:7

___

Master, thanks for Your power and authority to rescue me in my distress.

JANUARY 28

[10]I am the Lord your God, who brought you up out of Egypt. Open wide your mouth and I will fill it.

Psalm 81:10

Lord, my God, thank You for deliverance; being my God of love and truth.

JANUARY 29

[3]Who forgives all your sins and heals all your diseases.

Psalm 103:3

Father, thank You for Your forgiveness.

JANUARY 30

[10] He does not treat us as our sins deserve or pay us according to our iniquities.

Psalm 103:10

God, thank You for not giving me what I just deserve.

Prayre Jornnal for Young People

JANUARY 31

[12] As far as the east is from the west, so far has He removed our transgressions from us.

Psalm 103:12

Father, thank You for Your grace and mercy.

FEBRUARY 1

²For great is his love toward us, and the faithfulness of the Lord endures forever.

Psalm 117:2

Father, thank You for Your great faithfulness.

FEBRUARY 2

¹I lift up my eyes to the hills – where does my help come from? My help comes from the Lord, the maker of the heaven and earth.

Psalm 121:1

___

Master, all of my strength and help comes from You. I am blessed.

FEBRUARY 3

[10]My son, if sinners entice you, don't give in to them.

Proverbs 1:10

___

Lord, let me not entice anyone to sin. Grant me the wisdom not to sin.

FEBRUARY 4

[5]Trust in the Lord with all your heart and lean not on your own understanding; [6]In all your ways acknowledge him, and he will make your paths straight.

Proverb 3:5-6

_____
_____
_____
_____
_____
_____
_____
_____
_____
_____
_____
_____
_____
_____
_____
_____
_____
_____
_____
_____
_____
_____
_____
_____
_____
_____
_____
_____

Lord, with all of my heart, which You made, I will trust You to guide me and lead me.

FEBRUARY 5

[12] You will say, "How I hated discipline! How my heart spurned correction! [13] I would not obey my teachers or listen to my instructors.

Proverbs 5:12-13

___

Father, remind me that discipline is a result of obedience which is directly related to love. Lord, help me to increase my love by obeying more.

FEBRUARY 6

[4]Lazy hands make a man poor, but diligent hands bring wealth.

Proverbs 10:4

_____
_____
_____
_____
_____
_____
_____
_____
_____
_____
_____
_____
_____
_____
_____
_____
_____
_____
_____
_____
_____
_____
_____
_____
_____
_____
_____
_____
_____
_____

Father, keep me diligent in all my efforts. You have already given me the tools to achieve what I have asked.

FEBRUARY 7

[12] Hatred stirs up dissension, but love covers all wrongs.

Proverbs 10:12

Lord, unconditional love is the start of my Christian maturity. Thank You for my growth.

FEBRUARY 8

[14]Wise men store up knowledge, but the mouth of a fool invites ruin.

Proverbs 10:14

Lord, thank You for showing me how to speak and listen in proportion to the mouth and ears I possess.

FEBRUARY 9

[13] A gossip betrays a confidence, but a trustworthy man keeps a secret.

Proverbs 11:13

___

Father, I want my family and friends, my loved ones, to know that I am as trustworthy as You.

FEBRUARY 10

[14] For lack of guidance a nation falls, but many advisors make victory sure.

Proverbs 11:14

Master, thank You for allowing me the wisdom to seek counsel and advice.

FEBRUARY 11

[16] A kindhearted woman gains respect, but ruthless men gain only wealth.

Proverbs 11:16

Prince of Peace, help me gain respect, for to You I owe all of who I am.

Prayre Jornnal for Young People

FEBRUARY 12

[1] Whoever loves discipline loves knowledge, but he who hates correction is stupid.

Proverbs 12:1

Master, thank You for allowing me to escape stupidity.

FEBRUARY 13

[10]Pride only breeds quarrels, but wisdom is found in those who take advice.

Proverbs 13:10

Lord, take any prideful thing from me.

FEBRUARY 14

[30] A heart at peace gives life to the body, but envy rots the bones.

Proverbs 14:30

Father, let me not envy. Thank You for Your peace.

FEBRUARY 15

[7]Where a man's ways are pleasing to the Lord, he makes even his enemies live at peace with him.

Proverbs 16:7

___

Lord, let my ways be pleasing to You.

FEBRUARY 16

[3]The crucible for silver and the furnace for gold, but the Lord tests the heart.

Proverbs 17:3

Thank You, God for testing my love for You.

FEBRUARY 17

⁹He who covers over an offense promotes love, but whoever repeats the matter separates close friends.

Proverbs 17:9

Thank You, Father for the wisdom of love and of Your will and sacrifice.

FEBRUARY 18

⁸The words of a gossip are like choice morsels; they go down to a man's in most parts.

Proverbs 18:8

Thank You, Lord for my soul's wisdom and understanding.

FEBRUARY 19

[11] A man's wisdom gives him patience; it is to his glory to overlook an offense.

Proverbs 19:11

___

God, instill in me the ability to overlook anger.

FEBRUARY 20

⁷The lamp of the Lord searches the spirit of a man; it searches out his inmost being.

Proverbs 20:27

God, thank You for searching my heart and seeking my spirit.

FEBRUARY 21

There is no wisdom, no insight, no plan that can succeed against the Lord.

Proverbs 21:30

Lord, remind me that it is by Your grace that I am granted the desires of my heart; not by my own plan.

Prayre Jornnal for Young People

FEBRUARY 22

[1]A good name is more desirable than great riches; to be esteemed is better than silver or gold.

Proverbs 22:1

Lord, thank You for my name.

FEBRUARY 23

[15]Folly is bound up in the heart of a child, but the rod of discipline will drive it far from him!
Proverbs 22:15

Lord, thank You for Your discipline because of Your love.

FEBRUARY 24

[17]Do not gloat when your enemy falls; when he stumbles do not let your heart rejoice.

Proverbs 24:17

Lord, thank You for sparing me from failure. Let me remember Your commands.

FEBRUARY 25

[15]Through patience a ruler can be persuaded, and a gentle tongue can break a bone.

Proverbs 25:15

Father, I seek a gentle and loving tongue.

FEBRUARY 26

[16]If you find honey, eat just enough – too much of it, and you will vomit.

Proverbs 25:16

Father, dismiss the desire to overindulge in anything.

FEBRUARY 27

[21] If your enemy is hungry, give him food to eat; if he is thirsty, give him water to drink. [22] In doing this, you will heap burning coals on his head, and the Lord will reward you.

Proverbs 25:21-22

Father, giving to my enemy may be hard but it's harder not receiving from You. Create within me the desire to give.

… Prayre Jornnal for Young People

FEBRUARY 28

[17] As iron sharpens iron, so one man sharpens another.

Proverbs 27:17

Father, send me friends who will "sharpen" me in Your word.

FEBRUARY 29

[8]Speak up for those who cannot speak for themselves, for the rights of all who are destitute.

Proverbs 31:8

Lord, thank You for my example of Christ.

MARCH 1

[1]"Cast your bread upon the waters, for after many days you will find it again."

Ecclesiastes 11:1

_____
_____
_____
_____
_____
_____
_____
_____
_____
_____
_____
_____
_____
_____
_____
_____
_____
_____
_____
_____
_____
_____
_____
_____
_____
_____
_____
_____
_____
_____
_____
_____

Master, You have given me confidence not to worry about anything. You promised to return to me what You gave to me as Yours.

MARCH 2

[10]So then, banish anxiety from your heart and cast off the troubles of your body, for youth and vigor are meaningless.

Ecclesiastes 11:10

Lord, thank You for allowing me to release my anxiety, my burdens, casting them on You.

MARCH 3

[8]"For my thoughts are not your thoughts, neither are your ways my ways", declares the Lord.
Isaiah 55:8

___

Lord God, thank You for Your higher thoughts.

MARCH 4

[5]"Before I formed you in the womb I knew you, before you were born I set you apart: I appointed you as a prophet to the nations."

Jeremiah 1:5

_____
_____
_____
_____
_____
_____
_____
_____
_____
_____
_____
_____
_____
_____
_____
_____
_____
_____
_____
_____
_____
_____
_____
_____
_____
_____
_____
_____

Thank you Father for having a destiny preplanned for me.

MARCH 5

⁹The heart is deceitful above all things and beyond cure. Who can understand it?

Jeremiah 17:9

Lord, help me with my heart.

MARCH 6

[10]"I the Lord search the heart and examine the mind, to reward a man according to his conduct, according to what his deeds deserve."

Jeremiah 17:10

Father, show mercy when You reward according to my deeds and conduct, for I am not worthy of much.

MARCH 7

⁶"'O house of Israel, can I not do with you as this potter does?" declares the Lord. "Like clay in the hand of the potter, so are you in my hand, O house of Israel."

Jeremiah 18:5-10

Lord, thank You for molding and forming me. For I am Your piece of work.

MARCH 8

[11] Now therefore say to the people of Judah and those living in Jerusalem, "This is what the Lord says: Look! I am preparing a disaster for you and devising a plan against you. So turn from your ways and your actions."

Jeremiah 18:11

Thank You for offering me the opportunity to reform before casting punishment on me for my deeds.

MARCH 9

³⁹But I tell you, do not resist an evil person. If someone strikes on the right cheek, turn to him the other also.

Matthew 5:39

Thank You God for providing examples so we can have godly combat.

MARCH 10

[44]But I tell you: Love your enemies and pray for those who persecute you.

Matthew 5:44

Thank You Lord for the wisdom to love my enemies.

MARCH 11

[6]But when you pray, go into your room, close the door and pray to your Father, who sees what is done in secret, and will reward you.

Matthew 6:6

_____
_____
_____
_____
_____
_____
_____
_____
_____
_____
_____
_____
_____
_____
_____
_____
_____
_____
_____
_____
_____
_____
_____
_____
_____
_____
_____
_____
_____
_____
_____
_____

Thank You Lord for the reward of prayer.

MARCH 12

[13] And lead us not into temptation but deliver us from the evil one.

Matthew 6:13

Thank You Lord for the power of deliverance from evil and temptation.

MARCH 13

[14] For if you forgive men when they sin against you, your heavenly Father will also forgive you.

Matthew 6:14

Thank You, Lord for the promise of Your forgiveness through our deed of forgiveness of others.

MARCH 14

[25]Therefore I tell you, do not worry about your life, what you will eat or drink; or about your body, what you will wear. Is life more important than food, and the body more important than clothes?

Matthew 6:25

_____
_____
_____
_____
_____
_____
_____
_____
_____
_____
_____
_____
_____
_____
_____
_____
_____
_____
_____
_____
_____
_____
_____
_____
_____
_____
_____

Thank You, Father for commanding me not to worry and placing ease in my spirit.

MARCH 15

[33] But seek first His kingdom and his righteousness, and all these things will be given to you as well.

Matthew 6:33

Thank You, Father for showing me Your kingdom and offering me the privileges of Your kingdom and righteousness.

MARCH 16

[34] Therefore do not worry about tomorrow, for tomorrow will worry about itself. Each day has enough trouble of its own.

Matthew 6:34

Father, thank You for reminding me that You didn't create the spirit of worry.

Prayre Jornnal for Young People

MARCH 17

[1]Do not judge, or you too will be judged.

Matthew 7:1

Father, I come asking You for forgiveness for judging others that I may be spared from judgment by my own standards.

MARCH 18

⁷Ask and it will be given to you; seek and you will find; knock and the door will be opened to you.

Matthew 7:7

Father, thank You for the privilege of asking You anything and knowing that You will answer my prayers.

MARCH 19

[12] Do to others what you would have them do to you.

Matthew 7:12

God, thank You for treating me better that I treat others.

MARCH 20

[26]He replied, "You of little faith, why are you so afraid?" Then He got up and rebuked the winds and the waves, and it was completely calm.

Matthew 8:26

___

Lord, help me to increase my faith as I walk with You for this journey.

MARCH 21

[20] Just then a woman who had been subject to bleeding for twelve years came up behind Him and touched the edge of his cloak. [21] She said to herself, "If I only touch His cloak, I will be healed." [22] Jesus turned and saw her. "Take heart, daughter," He said. "Your faith has healed you." And the woman was healed from that moment.

Matthew 9:20-22

Lord, I find myself looking for the hem of Your garment.

MARCH 22

[39]Whoever finds his life will lose it, and whoever loses his life for my sake, will find it.

Matthew 10:39

Lord, thank You for saving my life.

Prayre Jornnal for Young People

MARCH 23

[28]"Come to me, all you who are weary and burdened, and I will give you rest."

Matthew 11:28

Thank You, God, for Your comfort.

105 | Minister Gage

MARCH 24

[27]But Jesus immediately said to them: "Take courage! It is I. Don't be afraid."

Matthew 14:27

Thank You for coming to me Lord, especially when I fear.

MARCH 25

²⁸"Lord, if it's you," Peter replied, "tell me to come to you on the water." ²⁹"Come," he said. Then Peter got down out of the boat, walked on the water and came toward Jesus.

Matthew 14:28-29

Even when I don't deserve to be shown, Lord you continue to show me that You are here as my Savior.

MARCH 26

[30] But when he saw the wind, he was afraid and, beginning to sink, cried out, "Lord, save me!"

Matthew 14:30

Jesus, thank You for allowing me access to call You when I deviate from Your plan.

MARCH 27

[31]Immediately Jesus reached out His hand and caught him, "You of little faith," he said, "why did you doubt?"

Matthew 14:31

Thank You for coming to me Lord especially when I fear.

MARCH 28

[15]"If your brother sins against you, go and show him his fault, just between the two of you. If he listens to you, you have won your brother. [16]But if he will not listen, take one or two others along so that 'every matter may be established by the testimony of two or three witnesses.' [17]If he refuses to listen to them tell it to the church; and if he refuses to listen even to the church, treat him as you would a pagan or a tax collector."

Matthew 18:15-17

___

Lord, teach me to avoid conflict but when I can't guide me as I attempt to resolve conflict in my life.

MARCH 29

[19]"Again, I tell you that if two of you on earth agree about anything you ask for, it will be done for you by my Father in heaven. [20]For where two or three come together in my name, there am I with them."

Matthew 18:19-20

___

Lord, thank You for granting me the requests of my loved ones and myself through group prayer.

On This Journey

MARCH 30

[37]Jesus replied, "Love the Lord your God with all your heart and with all your soul and with all your mind."

Matthew 22:37

Oh Lord, this the step that leads to a total love of You.

Prayre Jornnal for Young People

MARCH 31

[39] And the second is like it: "Love your neighbor as yourself!"

Matthew 22:39

Lord, teach me to always love my neighbor as myself.

DEVELOPING YOUR PRAYER LIFE— PART ONE

What is Prayer?
Prayer is your conversation to God and God's conversation to you. Prayer includes adoration, confession, thanksgiving, and supplication.

Each prayer will not be the same and will never include the same content. There is no "correct" prayer, so that means there is no "incorrect" prayer either. Prayer is your time to communicate and commune with God. There is no specific length of time to pray.

Prayer requires a few things though. Prayer requires desire to communicate with God. It also requires an honest approach to God. Prayer requires your initiative. Prayer does not require fancy words (Biblical vernacular) or the prayers of others.

Prayer can be intimidating. When your elders pray, you may think 'I want to pray like ___ _____.' You complete the blank, but God doesn't require that. Try to avoid being intimidated by prayer. God just wants your pure heart and your honesty.

Let's start with how to approach God. Your approach should be of reverence. We are first taught to bow our heads and close our eyes. Our posture for prayer should be respectful to God. Does this rule out praying and driving? No, because my heart is humbled and bowed, and my spirit desires me to pray to God. Often times your environment needs to be changed in order to offer Him your full respect and attention.

Your words. What do I say to God? I want Him to know I love Him. I want Him to know how grateful I am to Him for waking me up. I am really glad He healed my grandmother. I am really sorry I cheated on my test at school. All of these statements can be said to God just as they are and they can be said individually or collectively. These statements need not be dressed or nor added to.

Later, as you mature as a Christian, more content will be added to your prayer time. You will be able to release everything to God. Sometimes you will share with God almost immediately. Your prayer life means that you pray regularly and fervently (with intimacy and communion). You have started to develop your prayer life when prayer comes to your mind and heart without an outside reminder. You will also yearn to share with God. Your time with God becomes more and more important. This intimacy with God will grow the more time you spend with Him.

There will come to pass a day when someone will ask you to pray. This invitation then confirms your prayer life is active. If the invitation never happens, then you offer to pray—another signal that your prayer life is active.

APRIL 1

^{35}'For I was hungry and you gave me something to eat, I was thirsty and you gave me something to drink, I was a stranger and you invited me in, ^{36}I needed clothes and you clothed me, I was sick and you looked after me, I was in prison and you came to visit me.'

Matthew 25:31-46

Lord, thank You for showing me how to help those labeled "least of these brothers" when I really know that the "least of these brothers" could easily be me.

APRIL 2

[39]"My Father, if it is possible, may this cup be taken from me. Yet not as I will, but as You will."

Matthew 26:39

Lord, thank You for showing me Your will for my life. Father, thank You for sharing with me that my will is secondary to Your will. Always remind me that Your will be done.

APRIL 3

⁴²He went away a second time and prayed, "My Father, if it is not possible for this cup to be taken away unless I drink it, may your will be done."

Matthew 26:42

Lord, thank You for assisting me in submitting to Your will.

APRIL 4

²⁹And then twisted together a crown of thorns and set it on his head. They put a staff in his right hand and knelt in front of him and mocked him.

Matthew 27:29

Lord, remind me when I complain about outsiders ridiculing me that they persecuted You first.

APRIL 5

[29]But whosoever blasphemes against the Holy Spirit will never be forgiven; he is guilty of an eternal sin.

Mark 3:29

___

Lord, I always want to be forgiven. Thank You for Your graciousness.

APRIL 6

[36]What good is it for a man to gain the whole world yet forfeit his soul?

Mark 8:36

Lord, protect my soul from temptation which would forfeit my soul.

APRIL 7

[46]For whoever is not against us is for us.

Mark 9:40

Jesus, thank You for helping us to distinguish who is for us and against us.

APRIL 8

[41] I tell you the truth, anyone who gives you a cup of water in my name because you belong to Christ will certainly not lose his reward.

Mark 9:41

___

Thank You for reminding me to give, Lord.

APRIL 9

⁹Therefore what God has joined together, let man not separate.

Mark 10:9

God, I pray not to interfere in Your work.

APRIL 10

[43] Not so with you. Instead, whoever wants to become great among you must be your servant, [44] and whoever wants to be first must be slave of all.

Mark 10:43-44

Jesus, if I could be ¼ of the servant You are.

APRIL 11

[24]Therefore I tell you, whatever you ask for in prayer, believe that you have received it, and it will be yours.

Mark 11:24

Thank You, Father for giving me what I have asked.

APRIL 12

[25] And when you stand praying, if you hold anything against anyone, forgive him, so that your Father in heaven may forgive you your sins.

Mark 11:25

Jesus, thank You for showing me how to forgive myself and others.

APRIL 13

¹⁷Then Jesus said to them, "Give to Caesar what is Caesar's and to God what is God's." And they were amazed at him.

Mark 12:17

Lord, let us not be borrowers but lenders. Let us owe no one.

APRIL 14

[32]Love the Lord your God with all your heart and with all your soul and with all your mind and with all your strength.

Matthew 22:37, Mark 12:30

Lord, help me love You with my whole heart, soul, mind and with all of my strength.

Prayre Jornnal for Young People

APRIL 15

³⁰"I tell you the truth," Jesus answered, "today yes, tonight - before the rooster crows twice you yourself will disown me three times." 31But Peter insisted emphatically, "Even if I have to die with you, I will never disown you." And all the others said the same.

Mark 14:30-31

_____
_____
_____
_____
_____
_____
_____
_____
_____
_____
_____
_____
_____
_____
_____
_____
_____
_____
_____
_____
_____
_____
_____
_____
_____
_____
_____
_____

Jesus, remind me of Your knowledge and wisdom, especially when I have decided against the truth.

APRIL 16

[1b]"Lord, teach us to pray just as John taught his disciples."

Luke 11:1-4

Thank You for the power and privilege of prayer.

APRIL 17

⁹"So I say to you: Ask and it will be given to you; seek and you will find; knock and the door will be opened to you. 10For everyone who asks receives; he who seeks finds; and to him who knocks, the door will be opened."

Luke 11:9-10

_____
_____
_____
_____
_____
_____
_____
_____
_____
_____
_____
_____
_____
_____
_____
_____
_____
_____
_____
_____
_____
_____
_____
_____
_____
_____
_____

Lord, thank You for Your gifts and blessings.

APRIL 18

[28]"Suppose one of you wants to build a tower. Will he not first sit down and estimate the cost to see if he has enough money to complete it?"

Luke 14:28

___

Thank You for allowing the benefits to outweigh the costs of following You and being Your disciple.

APRIL 19

³³In the same way, any of you who does not give up everything he has cannot be my disciple.

Luke 14:33

Lord, remove the things in my life which prevent me from serving You.

APRIL 20

[4]"Suppose one of you has a hundred sheep and loses one of them. Does he not leave the ninety-nine in the open country and go after the lost sheep until he finds it?"

Luke 15:4

Thank You, God, for keeping and seeking each of us.

APRIL 21

⁸Or suppose a woman has ten silver coins and loses one. Does she not light a lamp, sweep the house and search carefully until she finds it? ⁹And when she finds it, she calls her friends and neighbors together and says, "Rejoice with me; I have found my lost coin."

Luke 15:8-9

Lord, let not my heart be far from You nor worship in vain.

APRIL 22

[15]He said to them, "You are the ones who justify yourselves in the eyes of men, but God knows your hearts. What is highly valued among men is detestable in God's sight.

Luke 16:15

Thank You, for being Jesus Christ and sacrificing for me.

APRIL 23

⁴⁰On reaching the place, he said to them, "Pray that you will not fall into temptation."

Luke 22:40

Lord, grant me strength to avoid sometimes overwhelming temptation.

APRIL 24

[62] And He went outside and wept bitterly.

Luke 22:62

Lord, I weep bitterly when I sin against You. Thank You for Your abundant forgiveness.

APRIL 25

[34]Jesus said, "Father forgive them, for they know not what they are doing."

Luke 23:34

Lord, my Father, forgive me for I know not what I do.

APRIL 26

[46] Jesus called out with a loud voice, "Father, into Your hands I commit my spirit." When He had said this, He breathed His last.

Luke 23:46

Lord, I know that my spirit is Yours and I commit all of it to You.

APRIL 27

⁶He is not here; He has risen!

Luke 24:6

Lord, thank You for rising for me. Thank You for being obedient and sacrificing for my life.

APRIL 28

[32] They asked each other, "Were not our hearts burning within us while He talked with us on the road and opened the scriptures to us?"

Luke 24:32

God, the more I know the more I want to know. Father I love You for increasing my desire to study Your word.

APRIL 29

³⁶While they were still talking about this, Jesus stood among them and said to them, "Peace be with you."

Luke 24:36

_____
_____
_____
_____
_____
_____
_____
_____
_____
_____
_____
_____
_____
_____
_____
_____
_____
_____
_____
_____
_____
_____
_____
_____
_____
_____
_____
_____

Father, thank You for granting me Your peace.

APRIL 30

[38]He said to them, "Why are you troubled, and why do doubts rise in your minds? [39]Look at my hands and my feet. It is I myself! Touch me and see; a ghost does not have flesh and bones, as you see I have."

Luke 24:38-39

Christ, thank You for I know Your word is true.

YOUR PERSONAL TESTIMONY

Why do you need a personal testimony? Better question, why do you need to share your testimony? Your testimony was designed to share with others. This personal encounter with God is designed to elevate them and their spirit to a new level where more growth and development can occur. Don't be surprised when you experience some growth and development, too.

When did you accept Jesus into your heart? When have you recognized God for being in your life and moving you to the right place? When had God done the opposite of what you asked but it was better than you expected? When has God simply provided you His peace?

Spend about 15 minutes writing the answers to these questions, while considering how you would share these answers and with whom you would share the answers.

On This Journey

MAY 1

[45]Then He opened their minds so they could understand the scriptures.

Luke 24:45

The power and dominion rest in Your hands, Father God such that You do the complex as well as the simple. Thank You.

MAY 2

[26]"I baptize with water," John replied, "but among you stands one you do not know. [27]He is the one who comes after me, the thongs of whose sandals I am not worthy to untie."

John 1:26-27

God, I am extremely privileged to be Your child. Your presence is powerful to me. I am so unworthy.

On This Journey

MAY 3

⁷Jesus said to the servants, "Fill the jars with water"; so they filled them to the brim.

John 2:1-11

Lord, Your divine timing is crucial to my blessings. I realize I must submit to Your timing.

MAY 4

[16]For God so loved the world that He gave His one and only Son, that whoever believes in Him shall not perish but have eternal life.

John 3:16

Thank You, God for Your extraordinary love.

MAY 5

[34]"My food," said Jesus, "is to do the will of him who sent me and to finish his work."

John 4:34

Lord, I pray to always crave Your food.

MAY 6

[35] Then Jesus declared, "I am the bread of life. He who comes to me will never go hungry, and he who believes in me will never be thirsty."

John 6:35

Father, thank You for allowing me to come to You and offering me Your comfort and strength.

MAY 7

[36] But as I told you, you have seen me and still do not believe.

John 6:36

God, increase my faith such that I can believe without seeing everything.

MAY 8

[37] All that the Father gives me will come to me, and whoever comes to me I will never drive away.

John 6:37

Jesus, thank You for accepting me and being my intercessor.

MAY 9

[38] For I have come down from heaven not to do my will but to do the will of Him who sent me.

John 6:38

Christ, thank You for reminding me of my purpose.

MAY 10

³¹To the Jews who had believed him, Jesus said, "If you hold to my teaching, you are really my disciples. ³²Then you will know the truth, and the truth will set you free."

John 8:31-32

___

Lord, thank You for the truth and the privilege to share it with those who don't know You.

MAY 11

[35] Jesus wept.

John 11:35

Lord, forgive me when I cause You to weep.

MAY 12

[14] Now that I, your Lord and Teacher, have washed your feet, you also should wash one another's feet. [15] I have set you an example that you should do as I have done for you. [16] I tell the truth, no servant is greater than his master, nor is a messenger greater than the one who sent him. [17] Now that you know these things, you will be blessed if you do them.

John 13:14-17

Lord, humble my heart and set aside my ego so that I may obediently serve You through serving others.

MAY 13

[15]"If you love me, you will obey what I command."

John 14:15

Lord, teach me to obey You so that when I say that I love You, You will hear me.

MAY 14

¹⁸"If the world hates you, keep in mind that it hated me first. ¹⁹If you belonged to the world, it would love you as its own. As it is, you do not belong to the world, but I have chosen you out of the world. That's why the world hates you."

John 15:18-19

Jesus, they haven't done anything to me, which they haven't done to you first. Thank You for taking me out of this world.

MAY 15

[7]But I tell you the truth: It is for your good that I am going away. Unless I go away, the Counselor will not come to you; but if I go, I will send him to you.

John 16:7

Christ, thank You for sacrificing so that I may have communion with the Father.

MAY 16

[33] I have told you these things, so that in me you may have peace. In this world you will have trouble. But take heart! I have overcome the world.

John 16:33

Christ, thank You for Your spirit and promises.

MAY 17

[4]I have brought you glory on earth by completing the work you gave me to do.

John 17:1-5

Lord, if only I could ever say, "Lord, I have done the work for which You sent me."

MAY 18

[17] For in the gospel a righteousness from God is revealed; a righteousness that is by faith from first to last, just as it is written: "the righteous will live by faith."

Romans 1:17

_____
_____
_____
_____
_____
_____
_____
_____
_____
_____
_____
_____
_____
_____
_____
_____
_____
_____
_____
_____
_____
_____
_____
_____
_____
_____
_____
_____

Lord, help me to be righteous and faithful.

MAY 19

[21]For although they knew God, they neither glorified him as God nor gave thanks to him, but their thinking became futile and their foolish hearts were darkened.

Romans 1:21

___

Lord, thank You for keeping me grateful.

Prayre Jornnal for Young People

MAY 20

[11]For God does not show favoritism.

Romans 2:11

Thank You for loving us all the same.

MAY 21

[23] For all have sinned and fallen short of the glory of God.

Romans 3:23

Lord, I know I embarrass You. Thank You for forgiving me anyway.

MAY 22

[7]"Blessed are they whose transgressions are forgiven, whose sins are covered.

Romans 4:7

___

Lord, thank You for covering my sins. Remove my desire to sin.

MAY 23

[8]Blessed is the man whose sin the Lord will never count against him.

Romans 4:8

Thank You for forgetting my sins, Lord.

MAY 24

[21] Being fully persuaded that God had power to do what he had promised.

Romans 4:21

I respect and love You because of Your power.

MAY 25

[5]And hope does not disappoint us because God has poured out his love into our hearts by the Holy Spirit, whom he has given us.

***Romans 5:5**_

Thank You, Lord for Your generous outpouring of love.

MAY 26

[8]But God demonstrates his own love for us in this: While we were still sinners, Christ died for us.

Romans 5:8

Lord, thank You for Your love – unconditional and abundant.

MAY 27

[23]For the wages of sin is death, but the gift of God is eternal life in Christ Jesus our Lord.

Romans 6:23

Thank You for Your gift.

MAY 28

[17]As it is, it is no longer I myself who do it, but it is sin living in me.

Romans 7:17

___

Lord, help me to overcome the sin which lives within me.

MAY 29

[18]I know that nothing good lives in me, that is, in my sinful nature. For I have the desire to do what is good, but I cannot carry it out.

Romans 7:18

Lord, I have an intense desire to do the right thing. Can You please help me succeed?

MAY 30

[19]For what I do is not the good I want to do; no, the evil I do not want to do – this I keep on doing.

Romans 7:19

___

Lord, intervene on my evil activity. Do everything in Your power to stop me from participating in evil.

MAY 31

[20]Now if I do what I do not want to do, it is no longer I who do it, but it is sin living in me that does it.

Romans 7:20

Lord, I want to depart from this sin which lives in me.

JUNE 1

[1]Therefore, there is now no condemnation for those who are in Christ Jesus.

Romans 8:1

Forgive me for me condemning myself, Lord.

JUNE 2

⁵Those who live according to the sinful nature have their minds set on what that nature desires; but those who live in accordance with the Spirit have their mind set on what the Spirit desires.

Romans 8:5

Lord, I want desperately to live with the Spirit's desires.

JUNE 3

[8] Those controlled by the sinful nature cannot please God.

Romans 8:8

Thank You, Lord for being You.

JUNE 4

[10]But if Christ is in you, your body is dead because of sin, yet your spirit is alive because of righteousness.

Romans 8:10

Christ, thank You for living within me.

JUNE 5

[26] In the same way, the Spirit helps us in our weaknesses. We do not know what we ought to pray for, but the Spirit himself intercedes for us with groans that words cannot express.

Romans 8:26

Holy Spirit, thank You for interceding on my behalf.

JUNE 6

[28] And we know that in all things God works for the good of those who love him, who have been called according to his purpose.

Romans 8:28

Lord, I love You. I want things to work together for me and I don't want to miss my purpose.

JUNE 7

³¹What, then, shall we say in response to this? If God is for us, who can be against us?

Romans 8:31

Thank You for being for me.

JUNE 8

[9] That if you confess with your mouth, "Jesus is Lord," and believe in your heart that God raised him from the dead, you will be saved.

Romans 10:9

Lord, thank You for Your gift of salvation.

JUNE 9

Do not conform any longer to the pattern of this world, but be transformed by the renewing of your mind. Then you will be able to test and approve what God's will is--his good, pleasing and perfect will.

Romans 12:2

Lord, I want to more closely align myself with You daily.

JUNE 10

[9]Love must be sincere. Hate what is evil; cling to what is good.

Romans 12:9

Lord, thank You for Your love.

JUNE 11

¹⁴Bless those who persecute you; bless and do not curse.

Romans 12:14

Lord, Your example of life is priceless to me.

JUNE 12

[15] Rejoice with those who rejoice; mourn with those who mourn.

Romans 12:15

Thank You, Father God for instilling within the spirit of compassion and empathy.

Prayre Jornnal for Young People

JUNE 13

[1]Everyone must submit himself to the governing authorities, for there is no authority except that which God has established. The authorities that exist have been established by God.

Romans 13:1

Lord, I owe it to You to obey the authorities that You have place before me, including my parents, my teachers, my supervisors.

JUNE 14

[13]Therefore let us stop passing judgment on one another. Instead, make up your mind not to put any stumbling block or obstacle in your brother's way.

Romans 14:13

Lord, let me help others as You have helped me.

JUNE 15

[5]So that your faith might not rest on man's wisdom, but on God's power.

1 Corinthians 2:5

Lord, thank You for Your power where my faith rests.

JUNE 16

[9]However, as it is written: "No eye has seen, no ear had heard, no mind has conceived what God had prepared for those who love Him."

1 Corinthians 2:9

Thank You God for the gifts You have for me.

JUNE 17

[10]But God has revealed it to us by His spirit. The Spirit searches all things, even the deep things of God.

1 Corinthians 2:10

Holy Spirit, thank You for revealing to me the things I need.

JUNE 18

[16] Don't you know that you yourselves are God's temple and that God's Spirit lives in you? [17] If anyone destroys God's temple, God will destroy him; for God's temple is sacred, and you are that temple.

1 Corinthians 3:16-17

___

Thank You, Lord for making me a temple and honoring me.

JUNE 19

⁵Therefore judge nothing before the appointed time; wait till the Lord comes. He will bring to light what is hidden in darkness and will expose the motives of men's hearts. At that time each will receive his praise from God.

1 Corinthians 4:5

Lord, remove the temptation to judge others. Let me not be judged by others.

JUNE 20

[7] For who makes you different from anyone else? What do you have that you did not receive? And if you did receive it, why do you boast as though you did not?

1 Corinthians 4:7

Thank You, Father for making me Your child, different from others; yet committed to You.

JUNE 21

[10]We are fools for Christ, but you are so wise in Christ! We are weak, but you are strong! You are honored, we are dishonored!

1 Corinthians 4:10

Lord, remind me to honor those who sacrifice to honor You.

JUNE 22

[12]We work hard with our own hands. When we are cursed, we bless; when we are persecuted, we endure it.

1 Corinthians 4:12

___

God, thank You for the strength and courage for being able to stand no matter what comes my way.

JUNE 23

[13]"Food for the stomach and the stomach for food" – but God will destroy them both. The body is not meant for sexual immorality, but for the Lord, and the Lord for the body.

1 Corinthians 6:13

Lord, Almighty, I commit my body, soul and spirit to You. I won't give away what belongs to You.

JUNE 24

[19] Do you not know that your body is a temple of the Holy Spirit, who is in you, whom you have received from God? You are not your own; [20] You were bought at a price. Therefore honor God with your body.

1 Corinthians 6:19-20

___

Christ, I owe You a pure body for all that You have sacrificed for me to have this body.

JUNE 25

²⁵Now about virgins: I have no command from the Lord, but I give a judgment as one who by the Lord's mercy is trustworthy.

1 Corinthians 7:25

___

Thank You for all who are committed to a virgin life.

JUNE 26

[34]And his interests are divided. An unmarried woman or virgin is concerned about the Lord's affairs: Her aim is to be devoted to the Lord in both body and spirit. But a married woman is concerned about the affairs of this world – how she can please her husband.

1 Corinthians 7:34

_____
_____
_____
_____
_____
_____
_____
_____
_____
_____
_____
_____
_____
_____
_____
_____
_____
_____
_____
_____
_____
_____
_____
_____
_____
_____
_____

Thank You for healthy marriages. They are gifts. Thank You for our time together.

JUNE 27

[13]No temptation has seized you except what is common to man. And God is faithful; He will not let you be tempted beyond what you can bear. But when you are tempted, He will also provide a way out so that you can stand up under it.

1 Corinthians 10:13

_____
_____
_____
_____
_____
_____
_____
_____
_____
_____
_____
_____
_____
_____
_____
_____
_____
_____
_____
_____
_____
_____
_____
_____
_____
_____
_____
_____

Father, thank You for allowing me to escape from sin and temptation.

JUNE 28

[23]"Everything is permissible" – but not everything is beneficial. "Everything is permissible" – but not everything is constructive.

1 Corinthians 10:23

___

Lord, help me avoid what's not beneficial or constructive.

Prayre Jornnal for Young People

JUNE 29

[24]Nobody should seek his own good, but the good of others.

1 Corinthians 10:24

Thank You for inspiring me to seek good for others. Father, this selflessness is by Your design.

JUNE 30

[32]Do not cause anyone to stumble, whether Jews, Greeks, or the church of God.

1 Corinthians 10:32

Lord, allow me not to cause anyone to stumble.

JUNE 30.5

[26] For whenever you eat this bread and drink this cup, you proclaim the Lord's death until He comes.

1 Corinthians 11:26

_____
_____
_____
_____
_____
_____
_____
_____
_____
_____
_____
_____
_____
_____
_____
_____
_____
_____
_____
_____
_____
_____
_____
_____
_____
_____
_____
_____
_____
_____

Father, thank You for returning for me.

DEVELOPING YOUR PRAYER LIFE— PART TWO

A component of prayer and a developing prayer life is intercessory prayer. This type of prayer is when you pray for others. Why don't they pray for themselves? Like yourself, they may not be able to pray for themselves or they don't know to pray or they may need some extra support.

A common intercessory prayer is one of salvation for someone who is not saved. But this type of prayer could include everything. When I am not about to see clearly my path or when huge decisions face me, I solicit the prayers of my prayer warriors and they pray for me. They may ask God for cover and protection. They may ask God for my increased wisdom about the issue. They may ask god to offer me His peace during whatever storm may be around.

Whatever they pray, they go to God in my place. In this instance, I am also still praying but I needed some help.

But when I need to be the intercessor? I prayed for my mother before I knew the definition, as did my grandmother. We were praying for the same reasons but at different levels. At six years old, my prayer probably followed this format:

"God, Mommy cries a lot and can't smile at me. She doesn't say much when drive home. She has a lot of marks on her body and when I ask, she gets really nervous. I saw Daddy hit her with a belt. Please make him stop. Amen."

When I was eight, they divorced, I was really sad initially because she still wasn't talking to me. I thought I had done something.

At age twelve, the prayer was 'thank You Lord for bringing my mother to church. I really like it that we go to church together.'

At 27, my prayer was 'thank You Lord for bringing Papa into her life and all that they experienced together. Now that he's with You, offer her comfort and peace and means for the rest of her journey.'

Intercession is bridging the gap between us and God. Intercession does not require the other's permission, nor do you have to tell them you prayed for them.

God sent the Holy Spirit, the third portion of the Trinity, to intercede for us. He petitions to God for us in many situations. The Holy Spirit has an assignment. Romans 8:26 reads, "In the same way, the Spirit helps us in our weakness. We do not know what we ought to pray for, but the Spirit Himself intercedes for us with groans that words cannot express." So when you don't know what to pray for, then know that the Holy Spirit is there interceding for you and each of your needs.

One last point about developing your prayer life. You will always mature in your walk and your prayer life will increase. Also, remember that prayer is daily and without ceasing. Try to avoid praying only when there is crisis. While God is all-powerful and performs crisis intervention daily, He does not prefer this method.

Your intimacy with God will reshape and mold and shape you to be more like Christ, the way He designed us—in His own image.

JULY 1

¹The body is a unit, though it is made up of many parts; and though all its parts are many, they form one body. So it is with Christ.

1 Corinthians 12:12

God, thank You for making us as a church function as one to achieve Your will.

JULY 2

[22] On the contrary, those parts of the body that seem to be weaker are indispensable, [23] and the parts that we think are less honorable we treat with special honor. And the parts that are unpresentable are treated with special modesty, [24] while our presentable parts need no special treatment. But God has combined the members of the body and has given greater honor to the parts that lacked it, [25] so that there should be no division in the body, but that its parts should have equal concern for each other.

1 Corinthians 12:22-25

Father, thank You for showing me how important each part of the body is to the whole.

JULY 3

^{26}If one part suffers, every part suffers with it; if one part is honored, every part rejoices with it.

1 Corinthians 12:26

_____
_____
_____
_____
_____
_____
_____
_____
_____
_____
_____
_____
_____
_____
_____
_____
_____
_____
_____
_____
_____
_____
_____
_____
_____
_____
_____
_____
_____

Lord, I come humbly to You thanking You for sharing with me how important we each are to You.

JULY 4

1 Corinthians 13

¹²Now we see but a poor reflection as in a mirror; then we shall see face to face. Now I know in part; then I shall know fully, even as I am fully known. ¹³And now these three remain: faith, hope and love. But the greatest of these is love.

Lord, thank You for proving Your LOVE to me and shining Your love through me.

JULY 5

⁵For God is not a God of disorder but of peace.

I Corinthians 14:33

God, remove from me what is disorderly for it is not of You.

JULY 6

[33] Do not be misled. "Bad company corrupts good character."

I Corinthians 15:33

_____

Lord, please warn me against bad character.

JULY 7

³Praise be to the God and Father of our Lord Jesus Christ, the Father of compassion and the God of all comfort, ⁴who comforts us in all our troubles, so that we can comfort those in any trouble with the comfort we ourselves have received from God.

2 Corinthians 1:3-4

Thank You for Your comfort and compassion.

JULY 8

[16]Therefore we do not lose heart. Though outwardly we are wasting away, yet inwardly we are being renewed day by day.

2 Corinthians 4:16

_____
_____
_____
_____
_____
_____
_____
_____
_____
_____
_____
_____
_____
_____
_____
_____
_____
_____
_____
_____
_____
_____
_____
_____
_____
_____
_____

Lord, remind me of my duty to share with others how You lift my spirit.

JULY 9

[18]So we fix our eyes not on what is seen, but on what is unseen. For what is seen is temporary, but what is unseen is eternal.

2 Corinthians 4:18

Lord, help me keep focused on the eternal.

On This Journey

JULY 10

[14]Do not be yoked together with unbelievers. For what do the righteousness and wickedness have in common? Or what fellowship can light have with darkness?

2 Corinthians 6:14

Lord, thank You for Your wisdom on friend and mate selection.

JULY 11

⁶Remember this: whoever sows sparingly will also reap sparingly and whoever sows generously will also reap generously.

2 Corinthians 9:6

Lord, open our hearts to be generous.

JULY 12

[3]For though we live in the world, we do not wage war as the world does.

2 Corinthians 10:3

Lord, forgive us for wanting to wage our own wars.

JULY 13

[9]But he said to me, "My grace is sufficient for you, for my power is made perfect in weakness." Therefore I will boast all the more gladly about my weaknesses, so that Christ's power may rest on me.

2 Corinthians 12:9

_____
_____
_____
_____
_____
_____
_____
_____
_____
_____
_____
_____
_____
_____
_____
_____
_____
_____
_____
_____
_____
_____
_____
_____
_____
_____
_____
_____

Father, thank You for Your grace and my weaknesses.

JULY 14

[19]The acts of the sinful nature are obvious: sexual immorality, impurity and debauchery; [20]idolatry and witchcraft; hatred, discord, jealousy, fits of rage, selfish ambition, dissensions, factions, [21]and envy; drunkenness, orgies and the like. I warn you, as I did before, that those who live like this will not inherit the kingdom of God.

Galatians 5:19-21

Lord, help me to avoid all sins daily.

Prayre Jornnal for Young People

JULY 15

²²But the fruit of the Spirit is love, joy, peace, patience, kindness, goodness, faithfulness, ²³gentleness, and self-control. Against such things there is no law.

Galatians 5:22-23

Lord, may we possess the fruit of Spirit.

JULY 16

[10]Therefore, as we have opportunity, let us do good to all people, especially to those who belong to the family of believers.

Galatians 6:10

Lord, help me serve them.

JULY 17

[4]But because of his great love for us, God, who is rich in mercy, [5]made us alive with Christ even when we were dead in transgressions – it is by grace you have been saved.

Ephesians 2:4-5

Thank You for Your grace.

JULY 18

[8]For it is by grace you are saved, through faith – and this not from yourselves, it is the gift of God – [9]not by works, so that no one can boast.

Ephesians 2:8-9

_____

Thank You for Your gift of grace.

JULY 19

[20]Now to him who is able to do immeasurably more than all we ask or imagine, according to his power that is at work within us.

Ephesians 3:20

Thank You for Your power working within me.

JULY 20

[23] Church, to be made new in the attitude of your minds.

Ephesians 4:23

Lord, prepare my mind for the greatness of my newness.

JULY 21

[24] And to put on the new self, created to be like God in true righteousness and holiness.
Ephesians 4:24

Thank You for my new self, God.

JULY 22

[26]"In your anger, do not sin." Do not let the sun go down while you are angry, [27]and do not give the devil a foothold.

Ephesians 4:26-27

Thank You, God for controlling my anger and limiting my sin.

JULY 23

[29] Do not let any unwholesome talk come out of your mouths but only what is helpful for building others up according to their needs, that it may benefit those who listen.

Ephesians 4:29

Father, monitor the words of my mouth.

JULY 24

[30] And do not grieve the Holy Spirit of God, with whom you were sealed for the day of redemption.

Ephesians 4:30

Lord, let me not grieve You.

JULY 25

[31]Get rid of all bitterness, rage, and anger, brawling and slander, along with every form of malice.

Ephesians 4:31

Lord, remove all forms of malice from me.

JULY 26

[32] Be kind and compassionate to one another, forgiving each other, just as in Christ God forgave you.

Ephesians 4:32

Lord, remind me at all to remain kind and compassionate.

JULY 27

[10] and find out what pleases the Lord.

Ephesians 5:10

Lord, help me know what pleases You.

JULY 28

[18]Do not get drunk on wine, which leads to debauchery. Instead, be filled with the Spirit.

Ephesians 5:18

Holy Spirit, please continue to fill me.

… Prayre Jornnal for Young People

JULY 29

[30] For we are members of his body.

Ephesians 5:30

And we are important to the body and I am grateful.

JULY 30

[1]Children, obey your parents in the Lord, for this is right.

Ephesians 6:1

Lord, remind me to be an obedient child.

JULY 31

²"Honor your father and mother" – which is the first commandment with a promise – ³"that it may go well with you and that you may enjoy long life on the earth."

Ephesians 6:2-3

_____

Lord, thank You for giving me parents to honor.

AUGUST 1

[4] Fathers, do not exasperate your children; instead, bring them up in the training and instruction of the Lord.

Ephesians 6:4

Lord, remind me to act gift-like at all times.

AUGUST 2

[11]Put on the full armor of God so that you can take your stand against the devil's schemes.

Ephesians 6:11

God, thank You for protection against the devil's schemes.

AUGUST 3

[13]Therefore put on the full armor of God, so that when the day of evil comes, you may be able to stand your ground, and after you have done everything, to stand.

Ephesians 6:13

Thank You, Father, for equipping me to stand my ground.

AUGUST 4

¹⁴Stand firm then, with the belt of truth buckled around your waist, with the breastplate of righteousness in place, ¹⁵and with your feet fitted with the readiness that comes from the gospel of peace. ¹⁶In addition to all this, take up the shield of faith, with which you can extinguish all the flaming arrows of the evil one. ¹⁷Take the helmet of salvation and the sword of the Spirit, which is the word of God.

Ephesians 6:14-17

Lord, with all this equipment surely I cannot fail nor falter.

AUGUST 5

[18] And pray in the Spirit on all occasions with all kinds of prayers and requests. With this in mind, be alert and always keep on praying for all the saints.

Ephesians 6:18

Lord, I cherish my prayer time with You.

AUGUST 6

[19] Pray also for me, that whenever I open my mouth, words may be given me so that I will fearlessly make known the mystery of the gospel.

Ephesians 6:19

Thank You, God for the power and privilege of prayer.

AUGUST 7

[24]whatever I need. Paul addresses God and requests grace for all who love the Lord Jesus Christ with an undying love.

Ephesians 6:24

Lord, sustain my love for You to an unconditional and undying level at all times and in all seasons.

AUGUST 8

[27]Whatever happens, conduct yourselves in a manner worthy of the gospel of Christ. Then, whether I come and see you or hear about you in my absence, I will know that you stand firm in one spirit, contending as one man for the faith of the gospel.

Philippians 1:27

Savior, regulate my conduct so that it is worthy of the gospel of Christ.

AUGUST 9

[28] Without being frightened in any way by those who oppose you. This is a sign to them that they will be destroyed, but that you will be saved – and that by God.

Philippians 1:28

Master, remind me that when I can take a stand for You that is the most popular response.

AUGUST 10

⁹Therefore God exalted him to the highest place and gave him the name that is above every name, ¹⁰that at the name of Jesus every knee should bow, in heaven and on earth and under the earth, ¹¹and every tongue confess that Jesus Christ is Lord, to the glory of God the Father.

Philippians 2:9-11

Lord, thank You for Your Son, the One above us all.

AUGUST 11

¹⁴Do everything without complaining or arguing.

Philippians 2:14

Father, remind me not to complain or argue.

AUGUST 12

⁶Do not be anxious about anything, but in everything, by prayer and petition, with thanksgiving, present your requests to God.

Philippians 4:6

Thank You, Lord for accepting my prayers and petitions to You.

AUGUST 13

[7] And the peace of God, which transcends all understanding, will guard your hearts and your minds in Christ Jesus.

Philippians 4:7

Thank You for Your peace, Lord.

AUGUST 14

⁸Finally, brothers, whatever is true, whatever is noble, whatever is right, whatever is pure, whatever is lovely, whatever is admirable – if anything is excellent or praiseworthy think about such things.

Philippians 4:8

___

Master, there are things which are noble, true, right, pure, lovely, admirable, excellent and praiseworthy. Lord, help me to see them each regularly.

AUGUST 15

[11]I am not saying this because I am in need, for I have learned to be content whatever the circumstances.

Philippians 4:11

_____
_____
_____
_____
_____
_____
_____
_____
_____
_____
_____
_____
_____
_____
_____
_____
_____
_____
_____
_____
_____
_____
_____
_____
_____
_____
_____
_____

Lord, mature me to contentment.

AUGUST 16

[13]I can do everything through him who gives me strength.

Philippians 4:13

God, with You, nothing is impossible.

AUGUST 17

[14]Yet it was good of you to share in my troubles.

Philippians 4:14

Lord, thank You those in my circle who are compassionate when I share my troubles.

AUGUST 18

[16]For by him all things were created: things in heaven and on earth, visible and invisible, whether thrones or powers or rulers or authorities; all things were created by him and for him.

Colossians 1:16

Lord, remind me when I forget why You created me.

AUGUST 19

²Set your minds on things above, not on earthly things.

Colossians 3:2

Lord, I want to keep my focus on You.

— Prayre Jornnal for Young People

AUGUST 20

⁵Put to death, therefore, whatever belongs to your earthly nature: sexual immorality, impurity, lust, evil desires and greed, which is idolatry.

Colossians 3:5

Master, I need help with the death of my earthly nature.

AUGUST 21

[10] And have put on the new self, which is being renewed in knowledge in the image of its Creator.
Colossians 3:10

Thank You for my new self and my increased knowledge.

AUGUST 22

[12]Therefore, as God's chosen people, holy and dearly loved, clothed yourselves with compassion, kindness, humility, gentleness and patience.

Colossians 3:12

Thank You for choosing me.

AUGUST 23

¹³Bear with each other and forgive whatever grievances you may have against one another. Forgive as the Lord forgave you.

Colossians 3:13

Father, allow us to better bear and forgive one another.

AUGUST 24

[14] And over all these virtues put on love, which binds them all together in perfect unity.

Colossians 3:14

Love is an action. Remind me, Lord to act in love.

AUGUST 25

[15]Let the peace of Christ rule in your hearts, since as members of one body you were called to peace. And be thankful.

Colossians 3:15

Lord, let me be peaceful and thankful beyond measure.

AUGUST 26

[16]Let the word of Christ dwell in you richly as you teach and admonish one another with all wisdom, and as you sing psalms, hymns and spiritual songs with gratitude in your hearts to God.

Colossians 3:16

___

Lord, I pray that Your word dwells in me richly daily with wisdom and sing with gratitude. Also, Lord, help me be the light You have called me to be.

AUGUST 27

[17] And whatever you do, whether in word or deed, do it in the name of the Lord Jesus, giving thanks to God the Father through him.

Colossians 3:17

Jesus, thank You for reminding me to do all I do in Your name.

AUGUST 28

[20]Children, obey your parents in everything, for this pleases the Lord.

Colossians 3:20

Obedience and honor to our parents represents our love for You. I want to love You with my whole heart, please help me, Lord.

AUGUST 29

[21]Fathers, do not embitter your children, or they will become discouraged.

Colossians 3:21

Lord, keep me encouraged.

AUGUST 30

[23] Whatever you do, work at it with all your heart, as working for the Lord, not for man.

Colossians 3:23

Thank You for showing me the depth of my heart.

AUGUST 31

[24b]Since you know that you will receive an inheritance from the Lord as a reward. It is the Lord Christ you are serving.

Colossians 3:24b

Thank You for my inheritance. Serving You is important to me. I will do it better.

SEPTEMBER 1

²Devote yourselves to prayer, being watchful and thankful.

Colossians 4:2

God, thank You for our time together.

SEPTEMBER 2

[5](Be wise in the way you act toward outsiders; make the most of every opportunity). Let your conversation be always full of grace, seasoned with salt, so that you may know how to answer everyone.

Colossians 4:5

Lord, allow the words of my mouth to be full of grace and wisdom.

SEPTEMBER 3

[11]Make it your ambition to lead a quiet life, to mind your business and to work with your hands, just as we told you.

1 Thessalonians 4:11

Lord, help me lead a quiet life, mind my business and provide me with more work with my hands.

SEPTEMBER 4

[12] So that your daily life may win the respect of outsiders and so that you will not be dependent on anybody.

1 Thessalonians 4:12

Lord, help me influence the lives of others through respect and independence.

SEPTEMBER 5

¹⁶For the Lord Himself will come down from heaven, with a loud command, with the voice of the archangel and with the trumpet call of God, and the dead in Christ will rise first.

1 Thessalonians 4:16

Thank You, Lord for coming to bring us to You as You promised.

SEPTEMBER 6

[17]After that, we who are still alive and are left will be caught up together with them in the clouds to meet the Lord in the air. And so we will be with the Lord forever.

1 Thessalonians 4:17

In Your presence is where I desire to be Lord. I look forward to being granted that privilege.

Prayre Jornnal for Young People

SEPTEMBER 7

¹²Now we ask you, brothers, to respect those who work hard among you, who are over you in the Lord and who admonish you. ¹³Hold them in the highest regard in love because of their work. Live in peace with each other.

1 Thessalonians 5:12-13

_____

Lord, let me not forget to respect those who work to increase my knowledge of You. Remind me that when I'm the teacher to exercise humility.

SEPTEMBER 8

[14]And we urge you, brothers, warn those who are idle, encourage the timid, help the weak, be patient with everyone.

1 Thessalonians 5:14

Lord, remind me to be kind and compassionate to those who need the kind and compassionate me.

SEPTEMBER 9

[15]Make sure that nobody pays back wrong for wrong, but always try to be kind to each other and to everyone else.

1 Thessalonians 5:15

Lord, I trust You to address those who wrong me and keep me kind to everyone.

SEPTEMBER 10

[16]Be joyful always.

1 Thessalonians 5:16

Even when it's hard, Lord, help me be joyful.

Prayre Jornnal for Young People

SEPTEMBER 11

[17]Pray continually.

1 Thessalonians 5:17

Lord, thank You for our open line of communication.

SEPTEMBER 12

[18]Give thanks in all circumstances, for this is God's will for you in Christ Jesus.

1 Thessalonians 5:18

Thank You, God for all of our circumstances.

SEPTEMBER 13

[19] Do not put out the Spirit's fire.

1 Thessalonians 5:19

God, I will help the Spirit's fire burn.

SEPTEMBER 14

[20]Do not treat prophecies with contempt.

1 Thessalonians 5:20

Lord, help me to believe Your words of prophecy through that of Your designated prophets.

SEPTEMBER 15

[21]Test everything. Hold on to the good.

1 Thessalonians 5:21

Lord, thank You for establishing what is good and giving me the ability to distinguish the difference.

SEPTEMBER 16

[22] Avoid every kind of evil.

1 Thessalonians 5:22

Lord, steer me away from and protect me from evil.

SEPTEMBER 17

[23] May God himself, the God of peace, sanctify you through and through. May your whole spirit, soul and body be kept blameless at the coming of our Lord Jesus Christ. [24] The one who calls you is faithful and he will do it.

1 Thessalonians 5:23-24

Thank You for Your great faithfulness.

SEPTEMBER 18

[6]God is just: He will pay back trouble to those who trouble you [7]and give relief to you who are troubled, and to us as well.

2 Thessalonians 1:6-1:7a

Thank You for taking care of me and paying back those who give me trouble.

SEPTEMBER 19

[10] For even when we were with you, we gave you this rule: "If a man will not work, he shall not eat."

2 Thessalonians 3:10

Lord, thank You for blessing me with work.

SEPTEMBER 20

[13] And as for you, brothers, never tire of doing what is right.

2 Thessalonians 3:13

Thank You for guiding my path and making it straight.

SEPTEMBER 21

[12] Fight the good fight of faith. Take hold of eternal life to which you were called when you made your good confession in the presence of many witnesses.

1 Timothy 6:12

Help me fight, God. Keep me fighting the good fight.

SEPTEMBER 22

[7]For God did not give us a spirit of timidity, but a spirit of power, of love and of self-discipline.

2 Timothy 1:7

Lord, thank You for Your power, love and the authority to act without timidity.

SEPTEMBER 23

[22]Flee the evil desires of youth, and pursue righteousness, faith, love and peace, along with those who call on the Lord out of a pure heart.

2 Timothy 2:22

___

Thank You, Father, for Your ability to pursue righteousness, faith, peace and love.

SEPTEMBER 24

[2]People will be lovers of themselves, lovers of money, boastful, proud, abusive, disobedient to their parents, ungrateful, unholy, [3]without love, unforgiving, slanderous, without self-control, brutal, not lovers of the good, [4]treacherous, rash, conceited, lovers of pleasure rather than lovers of God – [5]having a form of godliness but denying its power. Have nothing to do with them.

2 Timothy 3:2-5

Thank You for Your godliness and Its power.

SEPTEMBER 25

¹⁶All scripture is God-breathed and is useful for teaching, rebuking, correcting and training in righteousness, ¹⁷so that the man of God may be thoroughly equipped for every good work.
2 Timothy 3:16-17

Thank You for Your powerful word.

SEPTEMBER 26

⁶An elder must be blameless, the husband of but one wife, a man whose children believe and are not open to the charge of being wild and disobedient.

Titus 1:6

Lord, allow me to be worthy to lead among Your people as elder.

SEPTEMBER 27

[8] Rather he must be hospitable, one who loves what is good, who is self-controlled, upright, holy and disciplined.

Titus 1:8

Father, help me remain in Your favor by exhibiting these six behaviors and traits.

SEPTEMBER 28

[6]I pray that you may be active in sharing your faith, so that you will have a full understanding of every good thing we have in Christ.

Philemon 1:6

Savior, equip me to share my faith so others may know of Your love.

SEPTEMBER 29

⁷Your love has given me great joy and encouragement because you, brother, have refreshed the hearts of the saints.

Philemon 1:7

Master, remind me to bless others with my love.

SEPTEMBER 30

[13] To which of the angels did God ever say, "Sit at my right hand until I make your enemies a footstool for your feet"?

Hebrews 1:13

Lord, keep me humble in the face of my enemies.

READING GOD'S WORD

When you've heard your pastor or parents or other leaders say something and you thought 'wow', have you ever wondered how could they say that or know that or where did they get that from? Sure, we do. When I hear something of that magnitude, I look for it in God's word now. They can use God's word because they know God's words. They study the Bible and they read the Bible. They also realize that the Bible covers all subjects.

"How do I know what God's words say?" Read. Read. Read. Study. Study. Study. You must set aside time to read and study the Bible. If you start with 10-15 minutes per day, then you will increase that as you yearn more for His word.

"Where to start?" My suggestions are my favorite books: Matthew, Ephesians, James and Proverbs. Starting in any of these books will be easy. These books are an easy to read and understand. They also offer insight into your daily living and answers to your questions. Some books of the Bible require note taking, for me, especially with the names for ancestry and lineage. The history books of the Bible offer us information to understand the New Testament. The New Testament is not difficult but the more background you have, the better you will understand and deeper the meaning will be. For example, the prophets spoke of Jesus' birth, death and resurrection in the Old Testament. When He is born in the New Testament, John refers to the prophets of the Old Testament who spoke of His birth. Knowing this deepens your understanding for God's omniscience and omnipotence. Your knowledge will drive you to more knowledge. The more I know, the more I want to know.

"How do I find those great and special scriptures they know?" Spend time getting to know your sword (Ephesians 6:17). There are tools in your Sword to assist you in your study. The Bible has a table of contents and a key to assist you to understand the symbols used throughout the scriptures. In the front of each book, there is information and history given to clarify and provide background for the book. Included is usually a glossary and a concordance or index. The index allows you to use topics to find all scriptures related to the topic. There also some other quick reference resources, which assist you in answering your questions. These Bible helps are easy to follow and easy to use. You need to be consistent with your use.

Once you have read some more scripture, then you need to select a few scriptures to memorize. You memorize them by reading aloud, writing and repeating. Then apply it to your life, which will help you remember the scripture. Just a note, I once thought I couldn't remember scripture, but then I realized that I know the words to at least 50 songs, both Christian and secular, all of which are longer than a scripture.

It will help you to read more when you have a study partner. You will have accountability to your partner and vice versa. Spend time with His word. It's well worth your time.

God requires a tenth of what He has given us, so we have 2 hours and 24 minutes we owe to God daily. That time should be shared between reading and praying.

OCTOBER 1

[25] Therefore He is able to save completely those who come to God through him, because he always lives to intercede for them.

Hebrews 7:25

Thank You for saving me and interceding for me.

OCTOBER 2

²²Let us draw near to God with a sincere heart in full assurance of faith, having our hearts sprinkled to cleanse us from a guilty conscience and having our bodies washed with pure water.

Hebrews 10:22

Lord, draw me nearer to Thee.

OCTOBER 3

[24] And let us consider how we may spur one another on toward love and good deeds.

Hebrews 10:24

Lord, help me love others so that they may love others too.

OCTOBER 4

[26] If we deliberately keep on sinning after we received the knowledge of the truth; no sacrifice for sins is left, [27] but only a fearful expectation of judgment and of raging fire will consume the enemies of God.

Hebrews 10:26-27

Lord, give me the wisdom to stop deliberately sinning.

OCTOBER 5

[1]Now faith is being sure of what we hope for and certain of what we do not see.

Hebrews 11:1 (NIV)

[1]Now faith is the substance of things hoped for, the evidence of things not seen.

Hebrews 11:1 (KJV)

Thank You, God for increasing my faith.

OCTOBER 6

[1]Therefore, since we are surrounded by such a great cloud of witnesses, let us throw off everything that hinders and the sin that so easily entangles, and let us run with perseverance the race marked out for us.

Hebrews 12:1

Thank You, Lord, for keeping from some of the sin that so easily entangles us and thank You for marking our course for us.

OCTOBER 7

[10]Our fathers disciplined us for a little while as they thought best; but God disciplines us for our good, that we may share in his holiness.

Hebrew 12:10

Thank You Lord, for Your loving discipline and continual forgiveness.

OCTOBER 8

¹⁴Make every effort to live in peace with all men and to be holy; without holiness no one will see the Lord.

Hebrews 12:14

Lord. thank You for Your peace.

OCTOBER 9

[1]Keep on loving each other as brothers.

Hebrews 13:1

Lord, grow in us a brotherly love that endures.

OCTOBER 10

⁵Keep your lives free from the love of money and be content with what you have, because God has said, "Never will I leave you; never will I forsake you."

Hebrews 13:5

Lord, thank You for never leaving me in spite of who I'm not.

On This Journey

OCTOBER 11

⁸Jesus Christ is the same yesterday and today and forever.

Hebrews 13:8

Jesus, if I could be like You, then I would not waver.

OCTOBER 12

[17]Obey your leaders and submit to their authority. They keep watch over you as men who must give an account. Obey them so that their work will be a joy, not a burden, for that would be of no advantage to you.

Hebrews 13:17

Lord, remind me to be obedient to my leaders and allow those I lead to obey me.

OCTOBER 13

[18]Pray for us. We are sure that we have a clear conscience and desire to live honorable in every way.

Hebrews 13:18

Lord, each day I need to be renewed that I may live honorable in every way.

# OCTOBER 14

²Consider it pure joy, my brothers, whenever you face trials of many kinds, ³because you know that the testing of your faith develops perseverance.

James 1:2-3

Thank You for my joy. Thank You for my trials. Thank You for testing me.

OCTOBER 15

[4]Perseverance must finish its work so that you may be mature and complete, not lacking anything.

James 1:4

Thank You for grooming me to persevere anything.

OCTOBER 16

[5]If any of you should lack wisdom, he should ask God, who gives generously to all without finding fault, and it will be given to him.

James 1:5

Lord, thank You for Your wisdom.

OCTOBER 17

⁶But when he asks, he must believe and not doubt, because he who doubts is like a wave of the sea, blown and tossed by the wind.

James 1:6

Thank You for keeping Your word and knowing that I believe.

OCTOBER 18

[12]Blessed is the man who perseveres under trial, because where he has stood the test, he will receive the crown of life that God has promised to those who love him.

James 1:12

Christ, thank You for Your blessings and standing by me through these storms.

OCTOBER 19

[13] When tempted, no one should say, "God is tempting me." For God cannot be tempted by evil, nor does he tempt anyone.

James 1:13

Lord, help me resist and not be led into temptation.

OCTOBER 20

[19]My dear brothers, take note of this: Everyone should be quick to listen, slow to speak and slow to become angry.

James 1:19

Lord, thank You for teaching me to listen.

OCTOBER 21

[20]For man's anger does not bring about the righteous life that God desires.

James 1:20

God, I desire a righteous life so please help me avoid anger.

OCTOBER 22

[22]Do not merely listen to the word, and so deceive yourselves. Do what it says.

James 1:22

Lord, help me do what It says.

OCTOBER 23

[26]If anyone considers himself religious and yet does not keep a tight rein on his tongue, he deceives himself and his religion is worthless.

James 1:26

Christ, please help me keep a tight rein on my tongue.

OCTOBER 24

³If you show special attention to the man wearing fine clothes and say, "Here's a good seat for you," but say to the poor man, "You stand there," or "sit on the floor by my feet," ⁴have you not discriminated among yourselves and become judges with evil thoughts?

James 2:3-4

Lord, remind me not to judge or discriminate.

OCTOBER 25

[17]In the same way, faith by itself, if it is not accompanied by action, is dead.

James 2:17

Lord, I want my faith to live.

OCTOBER 26

[1]Not many of you should presume to be teachers, my brothers, because you know that we who teach will be judged more strictly.

James 3:1

Thank You, God for the gift of teaching.

OCTOBER 27

⁵Likewise the tongue is a small part of the body, but it makes great boasts. Consider what a great forest is set on fire by a small spark.

James 3:5

Let the words of my mouth be few and pure, Lord.

OCTOBER 28

[9]With the tongue we praise our Lord and Father, and with it we curse men, who have been made in God's likeness.

James 3:9

Father, bridle my tongue, when I choose to curse others.

OCTOBER 29

[16] For where you have envy and selfish ambition, there you find disorder and every evil practice.

James 3:16

Lord, remove any envy or selfishness. I don't want them in my spirit.

OCTOBER 30

[17] But the wisdom that comes from heaven is first of all pure; then peace-loving, considerate, submissive, full of mercy and good fruit, impartial and sincere.

James 3:17

Thank You for Your wisdom—it's purity, peace and sincerity.

OCTOBER 31

[18]Peacemakers who sow in peace raise a harvest of righteousness.

James 3:18

Help me to help peace exist, God.

NOVEMBER 1

[2]You want something but don't get it. You kill and covet, but you cannot have what you want. You quarrel and fight. You don't have, because you do not ask God.

James 4:2

_____

Father, thank You for hearing and answering my requests.

NOVEMBER 2

[3]When you ask, you do not receive, because you ask with wrong motives, that you may spend what you get on your pleasures.

James 4:3

Lord, purify my motives and keep me focused on You.

NOVEMBER 3

[17] Anyone, then, who knows the good he ought to do and doesn't do it, sins.

James 4:17

Jesus, thank You for being my conscious and my redeemer and my guide.

NOVEMBER 4

[11]As you know, we consider blessed those who have persevered. You have heard of Job's perseverance and have seen what the Lord finally brought about. The Lord is full of compassion and mercy.

James 5:11

Lord, thank You for Your compassion and mercy which enables us to persevere.

NOVEMBER 5

⁶Who through faith are shielded by God's power until the coming of the salvation that is ready to be revealed in the last time.

1 Peter 1:5

___

Lord, help me remain faithful.

NOVEMBER 6

[6]In this you greatly rejoice, though now for a little while you may have to suffer grief in all kinds of trials.

1 Peter 1:6

_____
_____
_____
_____
_____
_____
_____
_____
_____
_____
_____
_____
_____
_____
_____
_____
_____
_____
_____
_____
_____
_____
_____
_____
_____
_____

Lord, I know that I grow through my trials.

NOVEMBER 7

⁷These have come so that your faith – of greater worth than gold, which perishes even though refined by fire – may be proved genuine and may result in praise, glory and honor when Jesus Christ is revealed.

1 Peter 1:7

Thank You for honoring my faith and remind me to always give You the glory. I can at least start toward what You deserve.

NOVEMBER 8

[8] Though you have not seen him, you love him; and even though you do not see him now, you believe in Him and are filled with an inexpressible and glorious joy, [9] for you are receiving the goal of your faith, the salvation of your souls.

1 Peter 1:8-9

_____
_____
_____
_____
_____
_____
_____
_____
_____
_____
_____
_____
_____
_____
_____
_____
_____
_____
_____
_____
_____
_____
_____
_____
_____

Lord, I love You because You loved me first.

NOVEMBER 9

[13] Therefore, prepare your minds for action: be self-controlled, set your hope fully on the grace to be given you when Jesus Christ is revealed.

1 Peter 1:13

Thank You for preparing my mind for action.

NOVEMBER 10

[14]As obedient children, do not conform to the evil desires you had when you lived in ignorance.

1 Peter 1:14

Lord, help me remain obedient. Keep me away from evil.

NOVEMBER 11

¹⁵But just as he who called you is holy, so be holy in all you do, ¹⁶for it is written: "Be holy, because I am holy."

1 Peter 1:15-16

Jesus, help me to be holy.

On This Journey

NOVEMBER 12

[18] For you know that it was not with perishable things such as silver or gold that you were redeemed from the empty way of life handed down to you from your forefathers, [19] but with the precious blood of Christ, a lamb without blemish or defect.

1 Peter 1:18-19

_____
_____
_____
_____
_____
_____
_____
_____
_____
_____
_____
_____
_____
_____
_____
_____
_____
_____
_____
_____
_____
_____
_____
_____

Lord, remind me that I was saved at a great price.

NOVEMBER 13

²⁵But the word of the Lord stands forever.

I Peter 1:25

Thank You for Your everlasting word.

NOVEMBER 14

[20]But how is it to your credit if you receive a beating for doing wrong and endure it? But if you suffer for doing good and you endure it, this is commendable before God.

1 Peter 2:20

Lord, I'll suffer for You and Your will.

NOVEMBER 15

[24]To this you were called, because Christ suffered for you, leaving you an example, that you should follow in his steps.

1 Peter 2:21

Christ, reveal my calling to me.

NOVEMBER 16

[23] When they hurled their insults at him, he did not retaliate; when he suffered he made no threats. Instead, he entrusted himself to him who judges justly.

1 Peter 2:23

Lord, teach me to ignore their ignorant comments and insults.

NOVEMBER 17

[24]He himself bore our sins in his body on the tree, so that we might die to sins and live for righteousness; by his wounds you have been healed.

1 Peter 2:24

Christ, thank You for saving me.

NOVEMBER 18

[8] Finally, all of you live in harmony with one another; be sympathetic, love as brothers, be compassionate and humble.

1 Peter 3:8

Lord, help me follow Your commands.

NOVEMBER 19

⁹Do not repay evil with evil or insult with insult, but with blessings because to this you were called so that you may inherit a blessing.

1 Peter 3:9

Thank You for allowing me to ignore the evil and insults directed at me.

NOVEMBER 20

[14]But even if you should suffer for what is right, you are blessed. "Do not fear what they fear; do not be frightened."

1 Peter 3:14

Lord, thank You for the gift of distinction about what to fear.

NOVEMBER 21

[17]It is better, if it is God's will, to suffer for doing good than for doing evil.

1 Peter 3:17

Lord, I want to do Your will. Help me avoid evil.

NOVEMBER 22

[8] Above all, love each other deeply because love covers over a multitude of sins.

1 Peter 4:8

Lord, remind me to love deeply.

NOVEMBER 23

[10]Each one should use whatever gift he has received to serve others, faithfully administering God's grace in its various forms.

1 Peter 4:10

_____
_____
_____
_____
_____
_____
_____
_____
_____
_____
_____
_____
_____
_____
_____
_____
_____
_____
_____
_____
_____
_____
_____
_____
_____
_____
_____
_____
_____
_____
_____

Lord, remind me to use Your gifts according to Your will and purpose.

NOVEMBER 24

[12]Dear friends, do not be surprised at the painful trial you are suffering, as though something strange were happening to you.

I Peter 4:12

Lord, when my trials come, help me to be prepared.

NOVEMBER 25

[13]But rejoice that you participate in the sufferings of Christ, so that you may be overjoyed when his glory is revealed.

I Peter 4:13

Lord, I suffer so that You may be glorified.

NOVEMBER 26

[19]So then, those who suffer according to God's will should commit themselves to their faithful Creator and continue to do good.

1 Peter 4:19

Help me, Father, to continue to do good.

NOVEMBER 27

⁵Young men, in the same way be submissive to those who are older. All of you, clothe yourselves with humility toward one another because, "God opposed the proud but gives grace to the humble."

1 Peter 5:5

_____
_____
_____
_____
_____
_____
_____
_____
_____
_____
_____
_____
_____
_____
_____
_____
_____
_____
_____
_____
_____
_____
_____
_____
_____
_____
_____
_____
_____
_____

Lord, remind me to act with humility and act humbly.

NOVEMBER 28

[6]Humble yourselves, therefore, under God's mighty hand, that he may lift you up in due time.

1 Peter 5:6

Remind me of Your timing, Lord. Remind me not rush You.

Prayre Jornnal for Young People

NOVEMBER 29

[7]Cast all your anxiety on him because he cares for you.

1 Peter 5:7

Thank You for wanting my anxiety. Thank You for caring for me.

Minister Gage

NOVEMBER 30

[10] And the God of all grace, who called you to his eternal glory in Christ, after you have suffered a little while, will himself restore you and make you strong, firm and steadfast.

1 Peter 5:10

Thank You for Your grace.

DECEMBER 1

[3]His divine power has given us everything we need for life and godliness through our knowledge of him who called us by his own glory and goodness.

2 Peter 1:3

___

Thank You for supplying all of my needs and some of my wants.

DECEMBER 2

[4]Through these he has given us his very great and precious promises, so that through them you may participate in the divine nature and escape the corruption in the world caused by evil desires.

2 Peter 1:4

Thank You for keeping Your promises. Help me better keep Your commandments and my promises.

DECEMBER 3

⁵For this very reason, make every effort to add to your faith goodness and to goodness, knowledge; ⁶and to knowledge, self-control; and to self-control, perseverance; and to perseverance, godliness; ⁷and to godliness, brotherly kindness; and to brotherly kindness, love.

2 Peter 1:5-7

Lord, thank You for faith, goodness, knowledge, self-control, perseverance, godliness, brotherly kindness and love. I want to be in Your will.

DECEMBER 4

[8] For if you possess these qualities in increasing quantities in increasing measure, they will keep you from being ineffective and unproductive in your knowledge of our Lord Jesus Christ.

2 Peter 1:8

_____
_____
_____
_____
_____
_____
_____
_____
_____
_____
_____
_____
_____
_____
_____
_____
_____
_____
_____
_____
_____
_____
_____
_____
_____
_____
_____
_____
_____

Lord, help me be effective and productive as I serve You.

DECEMBER 5

⁹But if anyone does not have them, he is nearsighted and blind, and has forgotten that he has been cleansed from his past sins.

2 Peter 1:9

Lord, allow me not to be nearsighted nor blind.

DECEMBER 6

[10]Therefore, my brothers, be all the more eager to make your calling and election sure. For if you do these things you will never fall, "and you will receive a rich welcome into the eternal kingdom of our Lord and Savior Jesus Christ."

2 Peter 1:10-11

Thank You for preparing a place for me.

DECEMBER 7

[16]We did not follow cleverly invented stories when we told you about the power and coming of our Lord Jesus Christ, but we were eyewitnesses if his majesty.

2 Peter 1:16

Lord, thank You for Your plan and Your vision.

DECEMBER 8

[17]For he received honor and glory from God the Father when the voice came to him from the Majestic Glory, saying, "This is my Son, whom I love; with him I am well pleased."

2 Peter 1:17

Thank You for offering me Your gratitude.

DECEMBER 9

⁹If this is so, then the Lord knows how to rescue godly men from trials and to hold the unrighteous for the day of judgment, while continuing their punishment.

2 Peter 2:4-10

Lord, thank You for providing us with hope.

DECEMBER 10

[13] They will be paid back with harm for the harm they have done. Their idea of pleasure is to carouse in broad daylight. They are blots and blemishes, reveling in their pleasures while they feast with you.

2 Peter 2:13

Thank You, Father for taking care of me and protecting me from those who harm me.

DECEMBER 11

[14] With eyes full of adultery, they never stop sinning, they seduce the unstable; they are experts in greed – an accursed brood!

2 Peter 2:14

Lord, help me to avoid greed.

DECEMBER 12

[19]They promised them freedom, while they themselves are slaves of depravity – for a man is a slave to whatever has mastered him.

2 Peter 2:19

Lord, let me not be slave to anything or anyone.

Prayre Jornnal for Young People

DECEMBER 13

⁹The Lord is not slow in keeping his promise, as some understand slowness. He is patient with you, not wanting anyone to perish, but everyone to come to repentance.

2 Peter 3:9

Lord, thank You for Your slowness and keeping Your promises, promises I don't deserve.

DECEMBER 14

[11]Since everything will be destroyed in this way, what kind of people ought you be? You ought to live holy and godly lives.

2 Peter 3:11

Lord, help me live a holy and godly life.

DECEMBER 15

[14]So then dear friends, since you are looking forward to this, make every effort to be found spotless, blameless and at peace with him.

2 Peter 3:14

Thank You for Your peace, which transcends all understanding.

DECEMBER 16

[8] If we claim to be without sin, we deceive ourselves and the truth is not in us.

1 John 1:8

Father, help me admit my sins. Thank You for forgiving me of my sins.

DECEMBER 17

⁹If we confess our sins, he is faithful and just and will forgive us our sins and purify us from all unrighteousness.

1 John 1:9

Thank You for being faithful.

DECEMBER 18

[10] If we claim we have not sinned, we make him out to be a liar and his word has no place in our lives.

1 John 1:10

Lord, I don't want You to be a liar. I have sinned.

Prayre Jornnal for Young People

DECEMBER 19

⁵But if anyone obeys his word, God's love is truly made complete in him.

1 John 2:5

Lord, I want to obey You. All the time.

Minister Gage

DECEMBER 20

⁹Anyone who claims to be in the light but hates his brother is still in the darkness. ¹⁰Whoever loves his brother lives in the light, and there is nothing in him to make him stumble. ¹¹But whoever hates his brother is in the darkness and walks around in the darkness; he does not know where he is going, because the darkness has blinded him.

1 John 2:9-11

Lord, help me not to hate.

DECEMBER 21

[15]Do not love the world or anything in the world. If anyone loves the world, the love of the Father is not in him. [16]For everything in the world – the cravings of a sinful man, the lust of his eyes and the boastings of what he has and does – comes not from the Father but from the world. [17]The world and its desires pass away, but the man who does the will of God lives forever.

1 John 2:15-17

Lord, let me love You the way You are supposed to be loved.

DECEMBER 22

[3] Everyone who has this hope in him purifies himself, just as he is pure.

1 John 3:3

Help me remain pure, Lord.

DECEMBER 23

⁶No one who lives in him keeps on sinning. No one who continues to sin has either seen him or known him.

1 John 3:6

Father, help me to be honest about my sins when I confess them to You.

DECEMBER 24

⁹No one who is born of God will continue to sin, because God's seed remains in him; he cannot go on sinning, because he has been born of God.

1 John 3:9

I will remain in You at all times and in all seasons.

DECEMBER 25

[17] If anyone has material possessions and sees his brother in need but has no pity on him, how can the love of God be in him?

1 John 3:17

Lord, let me answer and recognize You.

DECEMBER 26

[20]Whenever our hearts condemn us. For God is greater than our hearts, and he knows everything.

1 John 3:20

Lord, this is just one more exhibit of Your abundant love.

Prayre Jornnal for Young People

DECEMBER 27

[21]Dear friends, if our hearts do not condemn us, we have confidence before God [22]and receive from him anything we ask, because we obey his commands and do what pleases him.

1 John 3:21-22

Thank You for my confidence.

Minister Gage

DECEMBER 28

[4]You, dear children, are from God and have overcome them, because the one who is in you is greater than the one who is in the world.

1 John 4:4

I love you, Lord for You are greater than me, "them" and the world.

DECEMBER 29

[19]We love because he first loved us.

1 John 4:19

Thank You for loving me, God.

DECEMBER 30

[20]If anyone says, "I love God," yet hates his brother, he is a liar. For anyone who does not love his brother, whom he has seen, cannot love God, whom he has not seen.

1 John 4:20

Lord, let my love for them be clear because I want my love for you to be clear.

DECEMBER 31

[24]To him who is able to keep you from falling and to present you before his glorious presence without fault and with great joy –

Jude 24

While I don't deserve anything but death for my sins, I truly thank You for Your overwhelming forgiveness.

On This Journey

GOD'S ANSWERS TO YOUR PRAYERS

As a young Christian, you will ask 'how will I know when God has answered me?' I know I did. I wanted to know God's plan, strategy and answers for me and my life an to my prayers. Through my growth, I have learned that God has three answers: yes, no and wait.

Yes means you are granted your request. God has designed this for you at this time. God knows He can trust you with your request. No means your request is denied because His plans and your request don't match at this time. God doesn't have this in plans for you. Sometimes, His plans have something different and better for you (i.e. He gives you a car but it's a practical one rather than a sports car) and other times no means He doesn't want you to have it at all.

Wait means you are not ready for your own request. He doesn't deny me, but He tells me I'm not prepared for the responsibilities of my request. If I am granted my request and am not ready then, I any misuse or mistreat my gift.
> Thank Him as if your request has already been granted.
> Believe in your heart that God will grant your request and it will be yours.
> God's plans are better than any request you could ever so don't be disappointed when He says no
>> or wait even.
> Ask with the purest of motives and your request has a better chance.

My husband has a note, which reads "ask God for what you want but willing to accept what He gives you because it will be better than what you ask for."

God will answer you. He never leaves a prayer unanswered. We were approved for a home loan, but we applied for another home with another lender, who denied us. We later learned that the builder was dishonest and a poor craftsman. My husband had already thanked God for the rejection. God clearly answered us. He planned for us to be in one place but we tried to venture away. He made His plan clear. We obeyed.

Prayer is a powerful tool by which God and us are giving each other our undivided attention. We are focused on Him. He promises to hear our plea. He promises us peace for our burdens and for those of us who are burdened and heavy-laden. He promises to meet our needs. He promises to give us the desires of our hearts. God expects, and quite frankly deserves, glory for all of His goodness. For all of His mercy and grace.

A word of caution: be careful of asking why when things don't go your way. God's answer could easily be 'why not you?' Events occur to determine whether or not we can be trusted with God's work and gifts. Job is one example of what can happen to us and the best example of how we are to respond when things do happen.

Do not lose heart, God is working in our lives at all times. When He determines we are ready, He answers our prayers.

RESOURCES

FOR

THE JOURNEY

THE NAMES OF GOD

Elohim	The Creator
El Elyon	The God Most High
El Roi	God Who Sees
El Shaddai	The All-Sufficient One
Adonai	Lord, Master
Yahweh	Lord, Jehovah
Jehovah-jireh	The Lord Will Provide
Jehovah-rapha	The Lord That Healeth
Jehovah-nissi	The Lord My Banner
Jehovah-mekoddishkem	The Lord Who Sanctifies You
Jehovah-shalom	The Lord Is Peace
Jehovah-sabaoth	The Lord of Hosts
Jehovah-raah	The Lord My Shepherd
Jehovah-tsidkenu	The Lord Our Righteousness
Jehovah-shammah	The Lord is There
El Olam	The Everlasting God

THE PRAYER OF SALVATION

Salvation is defined by Random House as the act of saving or protecting from harm or loss. God provides salvation for us, His children, free of charge. In order to receive His salvation, we only have to accept Jesus as our Lord and Savior. Salvation is a gift, which we have nothing to earn and can do nothing to achieve. God planned salvation before He created each of us. The scriptures listed will show you God's plan and provision for your salvation. Then follows a prayer of salvation, which confesses your sin to God and will assist you in accepting God's gift of salvation.

Romans 3:10-12, 23	We are all sinners.
Romans 6:23	The penalty for sin.
Romans 5:8-9	The payment God made for sin.
Romans 10:9-10, 13	Confess Jesus as Lord.

Dear God: I know You love me. I realize I am a sinner. I have not lived as You have wanted me to live. I believe Your Son, Jesus, died for me on the cross and was raised from the dead to provide forgiveness and eternal life. Please save me as I turn from my sins, place my faith in Jesus and receive Him as Lord and Savior. I will no longer live according to my selfish desires and plans but will follow Your desires and plans for my life. Thank You for saving me and giving me eternal life. I pray this prayer in Jesus' name, Amen.

What do I about my family and friends who are not saved?
Your prayer for God to become Lord of their lives is critical. You have to pray for them diligently. You don't have to pushy. The Lord will handle the rest. You share with them what you know through your study and prayer and the Lord will do the rest. Invite them to your church. Don't be afraid to ask them about what they know and don't be afraid to share God with anyone, believers or not. Eventually, God will bring them to Him. Pray then watch Him work.

ADDITIONAL SOURCES FOR THE JOURNEY

Disciple Youth Bible
True Love Waits Bible
Worth the Wait by Tim Stafford
Choosing God's Best by Dr. Don Raunikar
The Five Love Languages of Teenagers by Dr. Gary Chapman
The 7 Habits of Highly Effective Teens Sean Covey
Love Letters to God From a Teenage Girl by Onedia Gage
The Notebook for the Christian Teen by Onedia Gage

INDEX

Genesis 1:3	23
Exodus 20:4-6	24
Exodus 20:7	25
Exodus 20:8-11	26
Exodus 20:12	27
Exodus 20:13	28
Exodus 20:14	29
Exodus 20:15	30
Exodus 20:16	31
Exodus 20:17	32
Numbers 6:24-26	33
Nehemiah 6:16	34
Nehemiah 9:6	35
Nehemiah 9:13	36
Psalms 3:4	37
Psalms 8:1	38
Psalms 46:1	39
Psalms 46:10	40
Psalms 54:2	41
Psalms 55:5	42
Psalms 55:16	43
Psalms 56:3	44
Psalms 62:1	45
Psalms 62:2	46
Psalms 63:1	47
Psalms 63:8	48
Psalms 81:7	49
Psalms 81:10	50
Psalms 103:3	51
Psalms 103:10	52
Psalms 103:12	53
Psalms 117:2	54
Psalms 121:1	55
Proverbs 1:10	56
Proverbs 3:5-6	57
Proverbs 5:12-13	58
Proverbs 10:4	59
Proverbs 10:12	60
Proverbs 10:14	61
Proverbs 11:13	62
Proverbs 11:14	63
Proverbs 11:16	64
Proverbs 12:1	65
Proverbs 13:10	66
Proverbs 14:30	67
Proverbs 16:7	68
Proverbs 17:3	69
Proverbs 17:9	70
Proverbs 18:8	71
Proverbs 19:11	72
Proverbs 20:27	73
Proverbs 21:30	74
Proverbs 22:1	75
Proverbs 22:15	76
Proverbs 24:17	77
Proverbs 25:15	78
Proverbs 25:16	79
Proverbs 25:21-22	80
Proverbs 27:17	81
Proverbs 31:8	82
Ecclesiastes 11:1	85
Ecclesiastes 11:10	86
Isaiah 55:8	87
Jeremiah 1:5	88
Jeremiah 17:9	89
Jeremiah 17:10	90
Jeremiah 18:5-10	91
Jeremiah 18:11	92
Matthew 5:39	93
Matthew 5:44	94
Matthew 6:6	95
Matthew 6:13	96
Matthew 6:14	97
Matthew 6:25	98
Matthew 6:33	99
Matthew 6:34	100
Matthew 7:1	101
Matthew 7:7	102
Matthew 7:12	103
Matthew 8:26	104
Matthew 9:20-22	105
Matthew 10:39	106
Matthew 11:28	107
Matthew 14:27	108

Matthew 14:28-29	109	John 6:38	155
Matthew 14:30	110	John 8:31-32	156
Matthew 14:31	111	John 11:35	157
Matthew 18:15-17	112	John 13:14-17	158
Matthew 18:19-20	113	John 14:15	159
Matthew 22:37	114, 129	John 15:18-19	160
Matthew 22:39	115	John 16:7	161
Matthew 25:31-46	116	John 16:33	162
Matthew 26:39	117	John 17:1-5	163
Matthew 26:42	118	Romans 1:17	164
Matthew 27:29	119	Romans 1:21	165
Mark 3:29	120	Romans 2:11	166
Mark 8:36	121	Romans 3:23	167
Mark 9:40	122	Romans 4:7	168
Mark 9:41	123	Romans 4:8	169
Mark 10:9	124	Romans 4:21	170
Mark 10:43-44	125	Romans 5:5	171
Mark 11:24	126	Romans 5:8	172
Mark 11:25	127	Romans 6:23	173
Mark 12:17	128	Romans 7:17	174
Mark 12:30	129	Romans 7:18	175
Mark 14:30-31	130	Romans 7:19	176
Luke 11:1-4	131	Romans 7:20	177
Luke 11:9-10	132	Romans 8:1	178
Luke 14:28	133	Romans 8:5	179
Luke 14:33	134	Romans 8:8	180
Luke 15:4	135	Romans 8:10	181
Luke 15:8-9	136	Romans 8:26	182
Luke 16:15	137	Romans 8:28	183
Luke 22:40	138	Romans 8:31	184
Luke 22:62	139	Romans 10:9	185
Luke 23:34	140	Romans 12:2	186
Luke 23:46	141	Romans 12:9	187
Luke 24:6	142	Romans 12:14	188
Luke 24:32	143	Romans 12:15	189
Luke 24:36	144	Romans 13:1	190
Luke 24:38-39	145	Romans 14:13	191
Luke 24:45	146	1 Corinthians 2:5	192
John 1:26-27	148	1 Corinthians 2:9	193
John 2:1-11	149	1 Corinthians 2:10	194
John 3:16	150	1 Corinthians 3:16-17	195
John 4:34	151	1 Corinthians 4:5	196
John 6:35	152	1 Corinthians 4:7	197
John 6:36	153	1 Corinthians 4:10	198
John 6:37	154	1 Corinthians 4:12	199

Reference	Page	Reference	Page
1 Corinthians 6:13	200	Ephesians 6:19	246
1 Corinthians 6:16-20	201	Ephesians 6:24	247
1 Corinthians 7:25	202	Philippians 1:27	248
1 Corinthians 7:34	203	Philippians 1:28	249
1 Corinthians 10:13	204	Philippians 2:9-11	250
1 Corinthians 10:23	205	Philippians 2:14	251
1 Corinthians 10:24	206	Philippians 4:6	252
1 Corinthians 10:32	207	Philippians 4:7	253
1 Corinthians 11:26	208	Philippians 4:8	254
1 Corinthians 12:12	210	Philippians 4:11	255
1 Corinthians 12:22-25	211	Philippians 4:13	256
1 Corinthians 12:26	212	Philippians 4:14	257
1 Corinthians 13	213	Colossians 1:16	258
1 Corinthians 14:33	214	Colossians 3:2	259
1 Corinthians 15:33	215	Colossians 3:5	260
2 Corinthians 1:3-4	216	Colossians 3:10	261
2 Corinthians 4:16	217	Colossians 3:12	262
2 Corinthians 4:18	218	Colossians 3:13	263
2 Corinthians 6:14	219	Colossians 3:14	264
2 Corinthians 9:6	220	Colossians 3:15	265
2 Corinthians 10:3	221	Colossians 3:16	266
2 Corinthians 12:9	222	Colossians 3:17	267
Galatians 5:19-21	223	Colossians 3:20	268
Galatians 5:22-23	224	Colossians 3:21	269
Galatians 6:10	225	Colossians 3:23	270
Ephesians 2:4-5	226	Colossians 3:24b	271
Ephesians 2:8-9	227	Colossians 4:2	272
Ephesians 3:20	228	Colossians 4:5	273
Ephesians 4:23	229	1 Thessalonians 4:11	274
Ephesians 4:24	230	1 Thessalonians 4:12	275
Ephesians 4:26-27	231	1 Thessalonians 4:16	276
Ephesians 4:29	232	1 Thessalonians 4:17	277
Ephesians 4:30	234	1 Thessalonians 5:12-13	278
Ephesians 4:31	235	1 Thessalonians 5:14	279
Ephesians 4:32	236	1 Thessalonians 5:15	280
Ephesians 5:10	236	1 Thessalonians 5:16	281
Ephesians 5:18	237	1 Thessalonians 5:17	282
Ephesians 5:30	238	1 Thessalonians 5:18	283
Ephesians 6:1	239	1 Thessalonians 5:19	284
Ephesians 6:2-3	240	1 Thessalonians 5:20	285
Ephesians 6:4	241	1 Thessalonians 5:21	286
Ephesians 6:11	242	1 Thessalonians 5:22	287
Ephesians 6:13	243	1 Thessalonians 5:23-24	288
Ephesians 6:14-17	244	2 Thessalonians 1:6, 7a	289
Ephesians 6:18	245	2 Thessalonians 3:10	290

2 Thessalonians 3:13	291	James 5:11	336
1 Timothy 6:12	292	1 Peter 1:5	337
2 Timothy 1:7	293	1 Peter 1:6	338
2 Timothy 2:22	294	1 Peter 1:7	339
2 Timothy 3:2-5	295	1 Peter 1:8-9	340
2 Timothy 3:16-17	296	1 Peter 1:13	341
Titus 1:6	297	1 Peter 1:14	342
Titus 1:8	298	1 Peter 1:15-16	343
Philemon 1:6	299	1 Peter 1:18-19	344
Philemon 1:7	300	1 Peter 1:25	345
Hebrews 1:13	301	1 Peter 2:20	346
Hebrews 7:25	302	1 Peter 2:21	347
Hebrews 10:22	303	1 Peter 2:23	348
Hebrews 10:24	304	1 Peter 2:24	349
Hebrews 10:26-27	305	1 Peter 3:8	350
Hebrews 11:1	306	1 Peter 3:9	351
Hebrews 12:1	307	1 Peter 3:14	352
Hebrews 12:10	308	1 Peter 3:17	353
Hebrews 12:14	309	1 Peter 4:8	354
Hebrews 13:1	310	1 Peter 4:10	355
Hebrews 13:5	311	1 Peter 4:12	356
Hebrews 13:8	312	1 Peter 4:13	357
Hebrews 13:17	313	1 Peter 4:19	358
Hebrews 13:18	314	1 Peter 5:5	359
James 1:2-3	315	1 Peter 5:6	360
James 1:4	316	1 Peter 5:7	361
James 1:5	317	1 Peter 5:10	362
James 1:6	318	2 Peter 1:3	363
James 1:12	319	2 Peter 1:4	364
James 1:13	320	2 Peter 1:5-7	365
James 1:19	321	2 Peter 1:8	366
James 1:20	322	2 Peter 1:9	367
James 1:22	323	2 Peter 1:10-11	368
James 1:26	324	2 Peter 1:16	369
James 2:3-4	325	2 Peter 1:17	370
James 2:17	326	2 Peter 2:4-10	371
James 3:1	327	2 Peter 2:13	372
James 3:5	328	2 Peter 2:14	373
James 3:9	329	2 Peter 2:19	374
James 3:16	330	2 Peter 3:9	375
James 3:17	331	2 Peter 3:11	376
James 3:18	332	2 Peter 3:14	377
James 4:2	333	1 John 1:8	378
James 4:3	334	1 John 1:9	379
James 4:17	335	1 John 1:10	380

1 John 2:5	381	1 John 3:20	388
1 John 2:9-11	382	1 John 3:21-22	389
1 John 2:15-17	383	1 John 4:4	390
1 John 3:3	384	1 John 4:19	391
1 John 3:6	385	1 John 4:20	392
1 John 3:9	386	Jude 24	393
1 John 3:17	387		

ACKNOWLEDGEMENTS

God, thank You for Your plans for me. Thank You for **On This Journey** and choosing me to complete Your project. **OTJ** has brought me to the next level. I just want to please You. Thank You for continuing to anoint me and to invest in me and my gifts, which keep surprising me. Thank You for loving and forgiving me.

Hillary, and Nehemiah, thank you for enduring my late nights, your ideas, the sounding board, the love and the support. Thank you for loving me, especially when I do nothing without a pen and a clipboard.

To my inner circle: keep me in your prayers. As one of you asked: "how do you match 2001-2002?" I responded you ask God. You know I have asked God for much, so for me much is expected.

To my guardian children: J. Zachary Williams, Myya and Myles Malone. May these words touch your life and may we able to see God in all that we do.

To Pastor & Mrs. Ralph D. West and The Church Without Walls. Thank you for loving us in your ministry and for praying for us.

To my prayer warriors and surrogate parents: Mr. & Mrs. Willie Brown, Rev. & Mrs. Dempsey Wells, Jr., and Mr. & Mrs. Cleveland Brent. Thank you for your prayers and your love. One day I will receive the wisdom you have—I pray.

ABOUT THE TEACHER

Minister Onedia N. Gage believes in the study of God's word. She wants youth to have the help she wanted and needed as a former youth so that you can grow with God. She hopes that you will seek God for a closer relationship so that you can have a closer relationship with your family and friends.

Her life philosophy is three – fold:
  A) "What have you done today to invest in your future?
  B) Reading is essential to your positive contribution to our community; and,
  C) "If not me, who? If not now, when?" She feels her time is best spent when youth benefit from her experiences.

Minister Onedia invites you to share her study at her retreats for couples. Minister Onedia would like to pray for and with you. Please contact her via email onediagage@onediagage.com
Via twitter @onediangage, on facebook.com/onedia-gage-ministries and phone 512-715-GAGE (4243).

On This Journey

Preacher ♦ Prayer Warrior ♦ Teacher

To invite Rev. Gage to preach, coach, teach, and pray, Please contact us at
@onediangage (twitter) ♦ onediagage@onediagage.com ♦
facebook.com/onediagage
youtube.com/onediagage ♦ blogtalkradio.com/onediagage ♦
www.onediagage.com

Publishing

Do you have a book you want to write, but do not know what to do?

Do you have a book you need to publish but do not know how to start?

Would publishing move your career forward?

Let us help

onediagage@purpleink.net ♦ www.purpleink.net

713.705.5530

512.715.4243

www.ingramcontent.com/pod-product-compliance
Lightning Source LLC
Chambersburg PA
CBHW080540230426
43663CB00015B/2652